GETTING THE Whole Truth

Interviewing Techniques for the Lawyer

BARRY ZALMA

INTRODUCTION BY CELESTE FIORE

AMERICAN BAR ASSOCIATION

Solo, Small Firm and General Practice Division

Cover design by Amanda Fry/ABA Design.

Printed in the United States of America.

24 23 22 21 20 5 4 3 2 1

Library of Congress Cataloging-in-Publication Data

Names: Zalma, Barry, author. | American Bar Association. Solo, Small Firm and General Practice Division, sponsoring body
Title: Getting the whole truth : interviewing techniques for the lawyer / Barry Zalma.
Description: Chicago : American Bar Association, 2020. | Includes bibliographical references and index. | Summary: "The purpose of this book is to help you learn how to get the truth about anything from anyone. The reader who applies the principles discussed in this book will learn the effectiveness of the science of the interview. Having acquired this, the reader will then apply the knowledge and techniques as an interviewer, gradually honing the science into a genuine art . . . the art of getting useful, truthful information"– Provided by publisher.
Identifiers: LCCN 2020009733 (print) | LCCN 2020009734 (ebook) | ISBN 9781641056830 (paperback) | ISBN 9781641056847 (epub)
Subjects: LCSH: Interviewing in law practice–United States.
Classification: LCC KF311.Z35 2020 (print) | LCC KF311 (ebook) | DDC 347.73/0504–dc23
LC record available at https://lccn.loc.gov/2020009733
LC ebook record available at https://lccn.loc.gov/2020009734

Discounts are available for books ordered in bulk. Special consideration is given to state bars, CLE programs, and other bar-related organizations. Inquire at Book Publishing, ABA Publishing, American Bar Association, 321 N. Clark Street, Chicago, Illinois 60654-7598.

www.shopABA.org

For my children and grandchildren,
Stephanie, Holden, Shaina, and Aiden Zalma
and Sophie Bella Ostroff,
who have made my life a joy.

Contents

Preface

The interview is an essential form of fact gathering for every type of human interaction. Interviews happen everywhere; they are performed by almost everyone. Interviewing is also an art, and the most effective interviews are conducted by those who are knowledgeable and skilled in this art.

Everyone has been interviewed. And everyone has, at some point in life, interviewed another person. Not everyone conducting an interview, however, has accomplished the desired outcome. One type of informal interview that we all have experienced or observed is the conversation between a parent and a child. Parents, as interviewers, are not generally as successful as we might often naturally assume. For example, a little boy rushes in the door red-cheeked and out of breath; his mother asks:

"Where have you been?"

"Out."

"What did you do?"

"Nothing."

The mother's information gathering could have yielded richer results if she had learned some of the basic techniques used by professional interviewers such as police officers or lawyers. Had the mother used such tactics, the interview might have gone like this:

"Where have you been?"

"Out."

"Where?"

"Outside."

"I see your clothes are wet. How did that happen?"

"Josh's friend, Willie, splashed me."

"Where was Willie?"

"In his tank."

"Tank?"

"You know, at the aquarium."

"Oh, yes. And you and Josh went to see Willie?"

"Yes, they are best friends."

"And Willie splashed you?"

"He was hungry, and as we held fish over the side of the tank Willie would come out of the water and take them from us. He's big, you know, and splashes."

"Does Willie work at the aquarium?"

"Of course not, Mom. Willie is a killer whale."

Many people, parents included, simply are not skillful interviewers. They usually obtain, as in the unsuccessful interview above, almost no information from the person interviewed. The unskilled interviewer mom confirmed only the obvious fact that her five-year-old son had been "out." The mom who was experienced and skilled at interviewing learned both *where* her son had gone and *what* he had done.

This simple example demonstrates the wider sense of the term *interview* as it is used in this book. Parents interview children, and children interview parents. Teachers interview students, and students interview teachers. Employers and employees interview each other, as do store clerks and customers, and all manner of people interacting socially. In this sense, anyone who wants to gain information from anyone else, in any context or situation in life . . . *interviews.*

Law school limits its efforts to teaching students the law. Interviewing and interviewing techniques are ignored. This is odd, since most of what a lawyer does is obtain information to resolve disputes, prepare contracts, prepare important documents, or present to a judge or jury. The purpose of this book is to teach the lawyer—whether a novice meeting his or her first client or a grizzled old trial lawyer—effective methods of obtaining information by human interaction.

Now more than ever, obtaining sufficient relevant information is imperative in everything a lawyer does to protect the interests of the client.

The lawyer with an engaging curiosity who consciously applies one or more of the techniques set out here will obtain far more information than any of his or her competitors who lack interviewing skills. Armed with more information, the lawyer can proceed to make intelligent decisions (or, in the case of the consulting lawyer, obtain sufficient information to allow his or her client to make better decisions) and can thereby profit from the knowledge gained. Lawyers who are incompetent interviewers will be far less successful in every walk of life, despite their determination and effort, and will often experience failure simply due to an inability to gain the necessary information in a systematic manner.

Information Is Indispensable

When Edward Lloyd opened his coffee shop in the shipping center of London in the seventeenth century, he recognized that having up-to-date and pertinent information was the essence of any successful insurance operation. Since the majority of his customers were in the shipping or insurance business, he astutely noted that if they were not sufficiently conversant with the ever-changing facts of their profession, they frequently lost their investments. Because Lloyd had the insight that his customers needed to be fully informed, he kept a chalkboard on which the latest intelligence concerning shipping at the port of London was then recorded. This chalkboard was on constant display in his coffee shop, and his customers—again, largely made up of shippers and insurance underwriters—could gather from the details posted on the board much of the information they needed to properly evaluate the risks their own customers were asking them to undertake.

As the insurance business grew (eventually to become Lloyd's of London), and as the people who bought insurance became more sophisticated, underwriters and the lawyers who represented them needed to gather and efficiently evaluate detailed information even more urgently. Of necessity, underwriters and the lawyers who represented them rapidly developed into very competent interviewers.

Insurers soon found, therefore, that they needed the services of trained investigators and lawyers before they could properly evaluate a risk or a claim. They learned that conducting even minimal research before taking a risk would save an otherwise enormously expensive investigation and litigation that could occur *after* a loss. To further this aim of evaluating and reducing risk, the lawyers who represented the underwriters at Lloyd's borrowed investigative interviewing techniques that had long been used by detectives at Scotland Yard, and they soon developed additional techniques unique to the insurance profession.

Other businesses soon realized the wisdom of the work of the insurance industry. Businesses faced with fraud, embezzlement, employee dishonesty, and competition also found that accurate information was necessary to operate effectively and was needed by their lawyers in presenting their cases in courts of law. Increasingly, in every type of entrepreneurial endeavor, especially in the practice of law, the gathering of intelligence relevant to the business and its field of competitors became essential.

Modern news organizations—wire services like Reuters and the Associated Press, radio and television networks such as CNN, Fox News, MSNBC, NBC, CBS, and ABC, and news websites that are Internet-based—were all designed to provide credible and useful information to those who needed it. News reporters, if they are to be effective, must be consummate interviewers. If news is not gathered in a reliable fashion by skilled interviewers, it will be useless, and the news organization will lose all credibility. Without the skill needed to obtain information from a witness or spokesperson—informally, or formally on a video or audio recorder—a news reporter could never put together a viable and believable story. Lawyers learned from the police and news organizations how to gather information to protect the interests of their clients. Whether in an informal first contact, a formal interview, a deposition, or a trial, the successful lawyer will apply the necessary techniques to gain needed information from a witness.

Gathering accurate information is as important to the lawyer and the client—whether an insurer, a retail sales organization, a manufacturer, a builder, an architect, an engineer, a physician, or even the corner grocery owner—as it is to an inquisitive parent who wants to know where their children have been and what they have done.

Lawyers who wish to be successful and effective interviewers must also understand that no interview technique works on everyone. Without the help of Erle Stanley Gardner, the fictional Perry Mason would never have obtained confessions by simply asking: "Isn't it true that you did the crime?" Confessions in a civil litigation are as rare as snowfall at the Equator or rain in the Gobi desert. The lawyer must know and understand how different types of people, with different backgrounds, different races, religions, national origin, or sexual orientation will react to a persistent questioner.

The purpose of this book is to help you learn how to get the truth about anything from anyone. The reader who applies the principles discussed in this book will learn the effectiveness of the science of the interview. Having acquired this skill, the reader will then apply the knowledge and techniques as an interviewer, gradually honing the science into a genuine art . . . the art of getting useful, truthful information.

Many inexperienced interviewers immediately assume that an individual is lying because he or she has a past criminal record or is from a particular racial group or is of a particular religion, or for any of thousands of other "reasons" founded in nothing more than the interviewer's personal biases. Every professional must avoid prejudice based on preconceptions about the interview subject, not simply as an obvious and positive egalitarian principle, but as anathema to conducting a successful interview. Everyone has prejudices, but the prudent professional recognizes this fact, places judgment "on hold," and keeps it out of any interview.

Interviewing as an Art Form

Professional interviewing intended to gather information is more than a practical skill; it can be seen as an artistic endeavor. The investigative interview conducted by a lawyer is a structured conversation between a trained and experienced lawyer and a person who likely has no training in, nor any real awareness of, interview procedures.

It is important to note here, from the start, that the interview is not an interrogation. It is not the stuff of spy films, police investigations, or prisoner-of-war camps. The art is developed from scientific techniques obtained from criminal investigators and trained psychologists, but it is performed by the proficient interviewer automatically, fluidly, and not self-consciously. In other words, the art of conducting an interview must have become so ingrained in the lawyer that it has become second nature. Experienced interviewers must be able to proceed without thinking about what they are doing, much as skilled typists do not think about their fingers while typing.

In the chapters that follow, I refer to people who gather information by means of the interview as "professionals." Most of the professionals referred to are lawyers. Some professionals do not necessarily have a degree or a certificate, and they certainly do not have any document conferring on them the title "Professional Interviewer."

Nevertheless, lawyer professionals are people who have raised the interview process to a veritable art combined with the science of the interview created over many centuries. King Solomon, as the Bible describes him, was a legal scholar, an ultimate judge, and a consummate interviewer. Lawyer professionals, like King Solomon, might also be described as those interviewers who are consistently able to obtain all potentially available knowledge, even if those being interviewed try to avoid revealing the information. Throughout this book, the terms *interviewer* and *professional* are used interchangeably, and the terms *person interviewed, subject,* and *witness* all refer to the interviewee in various contexts.

At times it may appear that this book has been written for police investigators, insurance investigators, or professional private investigators. Although this is not entirely the case, it is true that the art of uncovering the truth by a professional does draw heavily from the police sciences. This book is written for lawyers, who will often require the assistance and services of investigators and will need to apply the skills and techniques they learn with even greater ability than the investigators themselves.

Police interrogation methods derive equally from the study of human nature and from observations of the long practice of human conversation and the requisite skills of social interaction. Because these interrogations are formal and conducted in a confined space by a person in authority, the techniques used are far more limited than those used in a typical interview conducted by a lawyer. However, while a truly skilled professional interviewer can easily shift to being an equally effective interrogator, the opposite is rarely true. The only time the lawyer is involved in a structured interview is at trial when a judge controls the lawyer's questions. Therefore, it is always best to obtain the information and knowledge needed to present at trial before the trial begins.

All investigators and interviewers want their search for the truth to be thorough and accurate and to yield as much information as possible. However, criminal interrogations and civil interviews diverge in tone and substance. Although both are aimed at revealing the truth, they are used to reach different goals.

Police often seek a "confession," whereas interviewers seek information that will establish the truth. While this may seem too fine a distinction, the police are mainly concerned with ascertaining probability of guilt in a criminal investigation, whereas the professional is involved with multiple goals such as calculating risk, evaluating business opportunities, determining evidence to prove a tort or breach of contract, or obtaining information to prove a defense to claims or suits.

We can see the difference in the language used to describe these two forms of interview. For instance, an insurance lawyer will "take a statement" from a witness, while a police detective will "interrogate" the witness. A prosecutor will "cross-examine" a witness, while an insurance lawyer will conduct a prelitigation "examination under oath" or a "deposition." An Internal Revenue Service agent, certified public accountant, or certified fraud examiner will "audit" a suspected criminal's books, while an internal auditor will merely "review" those books and records.

We can find many examples in daily life that are just as illustrative. A mother will question her child out of curiosity about the child's activities, while an assistant principal will question the student to decide on an appropriate disciplinary action. A young man will seek information to find out if a particularly lovely young woman would make a compatible partner. And, for her part, the young woman will want to learn if the handsome young man has the moral character she wants in a potential mate.

Each of these individuals is doing the same basic thing: gathering information. The name given to the task, as well as the manner and tone the professional uses to gain that information, are the only differences. All are practicing, to lesser and greater degrees, the science—and the subtle art—of the interview.

Nothing but the Truth

The purpose of an interview is to uncover the truth; the method of uncovering the truth is the art of the interview. The standard interview does not have, nor should it be given, the pejorative tone conveyed by the expression "giving someone the third degree." Interview professionals do not use rubber hoses or hot lights, nor do they subject the interviewee to torture. In their limited arsenal, civil lawyers in practice do not have the power of the state, the reputation of the FBI, the majesty of a court trial, or the intimidation of a search warrant. All the civil lawyer has before litigation commences are intelligence, skill, wit, and persistence to obtain the information needed to protect his or her client.

Civil interviewing professionals are, therefore, compelled to get the information they need in the guise of a friend. They must be masters of the social graces; they must know how to put people at ease. The skill of the professional causes the person being interviewed to actually *want* to give information to the interviewer. When the interview is successful, the subject becomes a virtual *partner* with the professional in the effort to uncover the truth, the whole truth, and nothing but the truth.

This book is designed to help you become a professional interviewer. You may find some of the advice contradictory at times, but the art of the interview is as various as it is complex and subtle. One method can work smoothly with one personality type, yet make obtaining information impossible with another type.

A technique that works when interviewing a nervous person may prove totally ineffective with an angry subject or a "wise guy." You will function most effectively as an interviewer by learning to gauge and assess the personality of the person interviewed, and then applying, as appropriate, the tactics and techniques detailed here.

The techniques described here are intended to assist those who need to conduct successful interviews in all walks of life, will improve your interactions with clients, independent witnesses, colleagues, employees, and any human being with whom you come into contact. No matter whom you are seeking information from, or what your reason for desiring it, these techniques can help you meet and interact with others and effectively gather the facts you need.

Introduction: C Differences, Power Dynamics, and the Art of Interviewing

Celeste Fiore

You may find yourself surprised at all there is to gain from this book and the impact reading it will have on your life. The practice of law is not commonly thought of as scientific, but it actually deals with the science of people. The interviewing techniques and principles presented in this book reflect an implicit understanding that we must acknowledge differences in power dynamics, cultures, individual lived experiences, and a myriad of other social, cultural, and personal variables in order to obtain the information we need for our own practice of law.

Law has long been viewed as a subject in and of itself that can be boiled down and captured on paper, with law school curricula perpetuating this myth. We have ignored that our profession is centered in the interaction of people with one another, and with the larger systems those people create such things as courts, prisons, marriages, families, contracts, and insurance—along with a myriad of other topics from hornbooks to bar exam review courses. What we fail to acknowledge with any consistency is that law is not monolithic, existing separate and apart from social forces. The same way that there is not one culture in a country, the law in actuality is a convergence of complex societies and the systems created as products of people, and it is ever evolving.

Diversity, in all its dimensions, is a living feature of the practice of law today in the United States. That diversity requires us as legal ıtioners to be inclusion-mindful in our practice, whether it is our teractions with clients (actual or potential), colleagues, or even the courts. Yet there is still much work to be done collectively and individually when it comes to diversity and inclusion within the legal profession. Negotiation and interviewing classes—which practically consider other cultural approaches to communication and conflict resolution—have only recently been offered as electives for law students; a consideration of "minority" student recruitment and retention has closely paralleled the expansion of the legal canon. As a legal community, we have only begun to scratch the surface of the historical and current inequalities that our laws and we as practitioners of those laws perpetuate on our colleagues and our fellow humans.

Law is not an amorphous concept that expands easily to adapt and include but instead is a lived reality that accounts best for those in places of power and privilege. The people who have been or continue to be outside of the law, having their conduct, actions, and even private life decisions scrutinized and criminalized at a stricter level and higher rate, such as black people or LGBTQ+ people, are the ones who have known this to be true, whether in their experiences or in their hearts. The push-back and outcry about this exclusion from consideration and from justice is present in movements such as Queer Liberation and Black Lives Matter. These refusals to stand on the margins have brought attention to the fact that different people are disparately impacted by the laws.

As legal professionals, we have not necessarily been trained to consciously consider that the people we encounter might experience the world and the law differently than we do. Our clients and we ourselves may have unearned advantages such as white privilege, heterosexual privilege, and cisgender privilege that create blind spots in our thinking whose impact can be diminished through practice and training.

The first step is to consciously consider other people's differences: age, citizenship status, country of origin, employment status, ethnicity, familial structure, gender (including gender identity), marital status, race, region, religion, sexual orientation, socio-economic status, etc. This is not an exhaustive list but rather a good starting point of some of the main possible differences between interviewer and interviewee. Merely making a list of these differences forces us to acknowledge them.

The second step is to try to uncover whether those differences are relevant to a particular person or interview dynamic, in the least offensive manner possible. Active listening coupled with a bit of background research into a culture, religion, or experience with which you are not familiar can provide some baseline knowledge. For example, if you have information that you are interviewing an Orthodox Jewish or Muslim person, you may want to have someone of the same gender reach out to them and ask if they're able to speak with someone of a different gender alone or even with a chaperone. In this example, the potential interviewer/negotiator might need to be changed so that the interview can happen. It could be difficult to explain to your client why an interview needs to be rescheduled and a new interviewer prepped because you missed a gender issue stemming from a religious or cultural difference. Ask direct yet respectful questions such as, "In what language do you feel most comfortable expressing yourself" to a bilingual person. The results of the interview will be clearer and perhaps more thorough if conducted in the person's native language. These differences come with their power dynamics vis-à-vis the interviewer, that is, someone who is young might be intimidated by an older interviewer, which, if not recognized, could come across as deception.

The third step is to educate yourself on those differences and how they might play out. You can do your own research by finding texts, articles, or videos made by a specific community addressing an issue, to see what issues the community has already flagged for itself. Find a trusted colleague or other personal resource to ask direct questions that you might not be able to find an answer to or that feel very personal. For example, I have a colleague who I know I can ask about cultural norms or any other issues that someone from a Southeast Asian community might face. We must be able to swallow our pride and admit that we don't know it all in order to continue to learn.

The fourth step is to synthesize what you've learned in the first three steps. Be conscious and deliberate in analyzing how differences play out in interviewing or negotiation. To be fair, this not so much a step as a continuous process.

If you find that there are other factors related to a person's background or identity that need consideration to determine your approach, then you have acknowledged your privilege and have the opportunity to leverage it appropriately to ensure it does not stand in the way of you providing your client with the most meaningful representation possible. Utilizing the tools listed above, you can address the blind spots you might otherwise have had in your interviewing.

Diverse voices demand respect and show us how vitally important it is to have a colleague attorney or staff member who can appropriately approach that difference. Those of us existing in the margins of those larger systems have fought to have our voices heard, identities seen, lived realities recognized, differing experiences considered, and rights and safety protected. It is once a diverse voice has proved its usefulness that it is valued; however, by that logic we should understand that diversity has value already and should be steadfastly present and meaningfully included. Otherwise, opportunities of value are already being lost. If there are hypotheticals in this book that you find you do not understand or that you are not quite sure how to handle, you have implicitly acknowledged the value of diversity.

If your intention was not to learn about and absorb tools and thought processes to render you capable of helping to dismantle white supremacy, I apologize; you have been tricked into buying this book and now hold this possibility in your hands. If you are able to read this book and apply its principles to your legal work, you will also be capable of extending its lessons to your daily life. Put quite simply, this book invites the practice of empathy, and while such lessons are couched in terms of self-interest, they are there, nonetheless. In order to get what we, the interviewer, needs we must make an effort to understand the interviewee in order to meet them where they are. As you read this book, reflect on how cultural differences and power dynamics might impact interviewing, efforts that innately require empathy and an acknowledgement of disparities. Inherently, we know that we need to recognize and manage these differences in order to gain the information that we need. However, we don't always apply these same principles to our everyday life. Perhaps it is because it seems too difficult and tedious. Perhaps we think we need to be paid to do it. Perhaps there is something unsettling in using someone's differences to gain needed information. But is it really the other person's differences we are using, or is it we are being mindful of our differences? Or, perhaps the unsettled feeling we get is a manifestation of knowing that with just a little more practice or effort we could chip away at the privilege that keeps others down.

Interviewing requires an acknowledgement and appreciation of difference. If the interviewer assumes that the interviewee is just like them and refuses to strive for an understanding of a person's unique experience, information held will remain a secret. The secrets keep all of us back, even those who benefit from privilege. The realization that a fruitful interview necessitates understanding and acknowledgement of the disparate treatment of marginalized communities should plainly demonstrate the value of diversity and the ways the harms from systemic exclusion resulting from the social structural manifestations of white supremacy pose to justice. Using all the tools at our disposal such as those set forth in this book, we can take small yet conscious steps that both aid our clients and advance justice.

1

Interviews in Everyday Life

Interviewing is a part of everyday life. Whenever two or more people meet, information inevitably passes between them. Interviewing techniques are, therefore, used regularly by everyone. People quite casually and unconsciously use the interviewing techniques they have acquired and incorporated over time. Some rely on their innate compassion and natural curiosity; others prefer to prepare thoroughly for the interview encounter, even to the point of scripting; and still others conduct interviews and interactions with an aggressiveness that reveals their determination and purpose.

Our first important point in this book is to stress the simple tenet that effective conversationalists make skilled interviewers. Whenever any two people meet, they extract information from each other. When a spouse returns home from a long day at work, for example, his or her partner uses interviewing techniques not just to learn what happened during the day but to keep the loving relationship alive. The person who can effectively interview in daily life will succeed at obtaining the information needed to establish, maintain, or enrich a mutually beneficial relationship.

Love will bloom. Business will prosper. Respect will be engendered.

TWO PEOPLE MEET FOR THE FIRST TIME

Imagine, if you will, various strangers meeting at a social event. Perhaps it is a cocktail party attended by eager entrepreneurs and their prospective customers or two young lawyers hoping to be recruited by a large law firm. It could even simply be a family gathering where a matchmaking aunt has invited some unfortunate person she wants to introduce to her uncouth—and, consequently, unmarried—nephew. Meeting, conversing with, and learning about people at such events are essential to success in life, whether it be for future profit or for present human happiness.

Social gatherings, which generally do not have the benefit of applied interviewing techniques, produce limited conversations, such as the following:

"George, I'd like to introduce you to Martha."

"Hello, Martha, I'm pleased to meet you."

"Likewise."

"Can I get you a drink?"

"Sure."

Apparently, neither George nor Martha is familiar with interviewing techniques. Neither is likely to learn anything significant about the other by using such rote and minimal expressions. Each may even consider the other to be dull-witted or, at best, unsociable and unsympathetic. George delivers the drink and goes on to try in vain to communicate with others. Martha, having been unable to piece together a real conversation, gets no satisfaction from the encounter. The equally incompetent George moves from one person to another, never learning anything, never establishing a relationship that lasts past the obligatory handshake and the exchange of a few platitudes.

When interviewing techniques are consciously applied, the same first meeting might proceed as follows:

"George, I'd like to introduce you to Martha."

"Hello, Martha, I'm pleased to meet you."

"And I you. Are you in the widget business like our host?"

"No, I'm just Sam's cousin—the black sheep of the family. I practice insurance defense law."

"Really? I'm the risk manager for the Collins Widget Works, so I deal with many lawyers."

The two participants have made an opening. Martha and George are possibly on the way to a long and mutually satisfying conversation that could lead to a business relationship.

The difference between the two conversations is that the first is formalized but uninformative. The second reflects an honest interest by each person in the other. Each listens to what the other has to say and follows through with appropriate responses—including even a gently self-effacing attempt at humor—to ease the other into conversation. Both use real information (as opposed to stock phrases) to open up and continually widen the conversation, encouraging a friendly relationship.

Many people are shy at social gatherings, especially when they don't know most of the guests. They are embarrassed to ask strangers questions for fear they will be thought foolish or uninformed. They are wrong to feel this way, of course. It is always best to ask questions of strangers, if only for the fact that most people like nothing better than to talk about themselves. If an attitude of tentativeness (or even fear) is pervasive, the gathering will inevitably be unsuccessful. No one will learn anything about anyone else. Everyone will just stand around, sip their drinks, and ask themselves how they got dragged to such a non-event, not realizing that the real cause of their dissatisfaction and ennui is their lack of interviewing skills.

Hosts who want their gathering to succeed will invite people who understand interviewing techniques. Granted, hosts may not think in terms of "interviewing techniques" per se, but all hosts quite consciously invite people with good social skills. And those guests, in turn, may believe they are just being friendly, but they are in reality performing as model practitioners of the art of the interview. The more intelligent interviewers there are at the party, the more successful and enjoyable the event will be for all who attend.

Getting the Whole Truth

Human beings are social animals, and most people have a natural curiosity about others. Moreover, most of us believe in our own importance, and we are convinced that what we have to say is also very important. A good interviewer uses the trained ability to listen, and the natural tendency to be curious about others, to gain information and build on the developing conversation. To be effective, the interviewer must:

- ask questions that call for a narrative response.
- listen attentively to the response to each question asked.
- look directly at the person to whom the question is posed (eye contact conveys genuine interest and encourages a lengthier response).
- avoid questions that could produce "yes" or "no" answers lacking in information.
- always respond to inquiries with a reasonably detailed (not unduly long) narrative.
- repeat the cycle with good-natured enthusiasm and unflagging interest.

Unlike a police interrogation, a social interview requires a balance of information exchange: an equal sharing of speaking time and listening time. In the spirit of fairness that characterizes the social encounter, the interviewer must be ready to provide the other party with at least as much information as the interviewer receives. The sharing of information reflects the openness of the conversation and is the very basis of establishing a new relationship. When information is shared, each party understands that a bond of trust has been created, and each becomes increasingly willing to return the trust in kind.

A MANAGER MEETS WITH A SUBORDINATE

A manager who is inexperienced in interviewing techniques might meet with his subordinate and conduct an interview in the following manner:

> "Did you see to it that the widgets were delivered to Widget Enterprises?"
>
> "Yes."

This exchange conveys the basic information required but nothing more. If the manager wants to elicit more than a monosyllabic answer, the line of inquiry should follow a more skillful circuitous route:

"Wilson, I am concerned about Widget Enterprises."

"Why, boss? They're an excellent customer."

"That they are. We sell thousands of our widgets to them every year. It has been some time since we received a major order from them."

"But boss, we had an order last week, don't you remember?"

"No. Could you refresh my memory, Wilson?"

"Sure. They ordered 50,000 widgets to be delivered Tuesday morning. I had the staff work overtime to pack them for shipment and they left today, a day early. I called Widget Enterprises to tell them the 50,000 would be delivered by 8:00 a.m. Tuesday."

"That's wonderful, Wilson. Your initiative is what makes you so valuable to our company."

DRAW THE PERSON INTERVIEWED INTO NARRATIVE MODE

In the previous exchange, rather than a "yes–no" question that needed only a single-word response, the interviewer—in this case the boss—initiated an interview in which his subordinate was encouraged to give him a narrative response. This technique provided the manager with a complete response to his question about the state of the business relationship with Widget Enterprises, as well as pertinent details concerning how the recent order had been filled. The employee was eager to provide his boss with these specific details, thereby demonstrating that he had done everything his boss had wanted him to do. As a result, both the manager and the employee benefited from the exchange.

Getting Information from Subordinates

Management styles vary in ways that are as unlimited as the varieties of human personality. They can range from laissez-faire to micromanaging, from uninvolved and remote to "hands on" everything. Managers themselves come in all personality styles, ranging from the "ranting and raving" authoritarian to the "calm and collected" facilitator. A management style can be judged by the degree to which it creates and sustains an effective flow of essential information between management and subordinate levels, and by the degree to which that flow of information is emotionally (as well as practically) satisfying.

Getting Information from Supervisors

Similarly, a subordinate who wants feedback from his manager about his work performance and his position in the company could say:

"Boss, I've been here a year. Am I doing okay?"

"Fine, Wilson, just fine."

Wilson asked a "yes–no" question that left little room for narrative. Not surprisingly, he got a response that was less than the fully informative reply he was perhaps seeking. We know that a person who is suffering from the flu, feverish and sneezing, will often routinely answer "Fine" when asked, "How are you?" Was the boss merely being polite? Wilson's attempt at interviewing failed, and he learned little from the exchange.

If Wilson had applied basic interviewing techniques, the conversation could have gone more like this:

"Boss, I've enjoyed working here this past year."

"Glad to hear that, Wilson."

"I need your help, though."

"How might I help you?

"I keep trying to improve what I do for the company. Can you help me understand additional ways that I can do more for the company?"

"Wilson, it's been five years since anyone asked me that question. In fact, the last person to ask me that is now vice president! Let me give you some ideas. It may help you, and the company will certainly benefit, too."

Superiors don't like to give solicited testimonials to employees. They like even less being asked by an employee what duties need fulfilling, since the employer expects the employee to know the job and to carry it out without constantly seeking counsel. But a conscientious employee who expresses a genuine desire to take on more responsibility is so rare in business today that it will often cause a supervisor to take notice . . . to be more open and communicative with the subordinate. The attentive supervisor will feel it is in the company's best interest to take advantage of such evidence of a positive work ethic and dedication.

By asking for guidance and offering to do more for the company, the employee, Wilson, convinced his supervisor that he was the type of employee who takes a proactive interest in his job. Wilson, recognizing the needs of the supervisor in his role as a company representative, was able to engage his boss in a dialogue and draw a narrative from him.

The most effective interviewing technique in a business context is to draw the person being interviewed into a narrative by recognizing, and keeping in mind, the professional needs of that person.

TWO BUSINESSPEOPLE MEET

A lawyer is in business. Lawyers also represent people in business. Businesspeople meet for a variety of reasons, but most of the reasons concern buying, selling, and otherwise striving to make a profit from their association, and they often seek the assistance and advice of counsel at a business meeting. Information must pass between businesspeople in order for them to clearly understand each other's needs. Both sides work to secure the assurance that the business relationship will be profitable.

In the business world, as elsewhere, effective interviewing requires patience and skill. When two newly acquainted businesspersons want something from each other, both are initially concerned that sharing information may put them at a disadvantage. As we have seen, direct "yes–no" questions—like those required in a court of law—will often elicit only single-word responses, while the narrative-seeking technique takes a great deal of time. A lawyer understands the difference between an interview and testimony in court. The limitation on the type of questioning in a trial may be one reason court trials are so lengthy and drawn out—the courts frown on questions calling for a narrative. In any case, initial meetings between two businesspeople run the risk of being strained if patience and interviewing skills are not applied. The lawyer can help the businessperson by working together to obtain narrative responses after establishing rapport.

Make a Concerted Effort to Establish Initial Rapport

Building rapport is a fundamental aspect of all human communication and a basic element of social intelligence. In any first meeting, the interviewer (when in the role of the person seeking a relationship), whether a lawyer seeking clients or a businessperson seeking business, should avoid making overt or direct requests for business. The professional should first spend time establishing the necessary rapport and building the confidence of the person being interviewed.

In order to create genuine rapport as an interviewer, you should strive to:

- build trust by demonstrating honesty, reliability, and fairness, and by expressing an understanding of the other's views;
- show respect by maintaining a polite manner and expressing gratitude; and
- make yourself likable in your willingness to be empathetic.

Rapport is most often an in-person phenomenon, marked by harmony, accord, or affinity. A sense of rapport can be initiated by something as simple as the professional sincerely admiring the office décor. If, however, the meeting is relegated to a drab cubicle, rapport can equally be established by the professional commiserating about the difficulty of working in less than comfortable surroundings. Any expression of empathy will be appreciated by the person being interviewed and will quickly help establish that critical first platform of rapport.

Similarly, the professional should delay questioning the interviewee about the matter at hand and should instead first attempt to find mutual interests and concerns. To this end, subtle observations at the first meeting are essential. For example, a small child's drawing pinned to the interviewer's wall or taped to a computer tower can be a quick tool for establishing rapport. Noting the drawing, the professional and interviewee could both be induced to express the joy they feel about their children, thereby establishing genuine common ground.

Or, in another scenario, glimpsing a bowling trophy can start a conversation about recreational sports. A framed certificate from an educational association or professional organization may start a conversation about similar training or experience the professional has in common with the interviewee.

The task of establishing rapport can take only a few minutes, or it can take much longer. To complete a successful interview, it is imperative to allocate sufficient time to establish rapport before launching into the serious and detailed "business" part of any interview. Regardless of the professional's interviewing skills, if the interviewer does not first establish some degree of rapport, the goal of the interview will likely not be reached. Establishing initial rapport, though itself one of the key interviewing skills, is one that lawyers often ignore.

Simply put, people who have experiences in common will tend to identify with each other; people who identify with each other are often inclined to like each other; and people who like each other will tend to talk freely. Once an easy rapport has been established and each person understands that the other is not intimidating in any way but is, rather, *familiar*, conversation becomes much less guarded and information begins to flow freely. Business can now be conducted, and the interview can proceed to its successful completion.

A CHAIRPERSON ADDRESSES A BOARD OF DIRECTORS

A board chairperson has the option of demanding responses from company directors. The wise executive, following the advice and counsel of an attorney, knows better than to place corporate directors in the hot seat. It is more important that those directors be continually supportive, cooperative, and forthcoming with vital, instructive information. The skilled chairperson leads the board into conducting thorough discussions, using his or her power only to guide the discussion and subtly maintain control over the proceedings. Instead of posing demands, he or she leads a discussion.

The dictatorial chairperson of a widget manufacturing company might address the board in the following manner:

"What was our net profit this month, Johnson?"

"Six million five hundred thousand dollars, ma'am."

The information is received, but little else is learned.

The chairperson who is able to apply interviewing techniques will address the board much differently. For example, to initiate a conversation, the chairperson might say:

"What developments have transpired in the last month? . . . Johnson?"

"Our engineers have developed a whosiss that allows our widget to outperform by 20% the widgets manufactured by Unwidget Enterprises."

"What will this development cost the company?"

"That's the beauty of the whosiss. It actually reduces the cost of producing our widgets."

"Have you explained the whosiss to any of our customers?"

"Yes, several."

"What did they say?"

This draws out an informative and narrative response.

The chairperson could also ask:

"What is sales saying about this?"

"My staff in sales advises that the improvement will increase our sales by 40% if we don't change our pricing and 50% if we reduce our pricing to reflect our reduced costs of production."

"What would you say is the projected effect on net profit?"

"Well, ma'am, our figures show . . ."

The chairperson, by drawing out the board member, has learned of an important development. Johnson may not have intended to mention the "whosiss." In fact, he may never have found an opportunity to tell the chairperson about the "whosiss" if he had not been asked in a way that was designed to elicit a narrative response. The board would have been deprived of a sense of leadership, and profits may have suffered because information was kept from the executive.

Meetings conducted this way take time, but in the long run fruitful discussion is far more valuable than quick checklists and short-cut demands. With the information gained by allowing a member of the board to talk about the development at length, the chairperson will be able to evaluate pricing, estimate sales projections, and calculate the effect a reduction in price due to a technological advance might have on net profits.

A lawyer representing a business will similarly assist the CEO by using his or her skill as an interviewer to obtain the information needed from the board of directors, officers, and directors of the company, as well as all employees or supervisors asked to be part of the meeting.

A SPOUSE RETURNS HOME FROM A LONG DAY AT WORK

Long-term couples, because of their long familiarity with each other, often fail to communicate consistently or well. After many years together, conversation can become truncated and limited. The lack of communication will often drive couples to lawyers for advice. The lawyer's interviewing skill can help the couple stay together and avoid the expense of divorce.

The limited communication is usually not due to a lack of love for, or interest in, each other. It stems from the partners' mistaken feeling that they are so familiar with each other that voicing their concerns or expressing their interests is no longer necessary.

A couple who have been married 10 years may communicate like this:

"Welcome home, dear."

"Hi, what's for dinner?"

"Pot roast."

"Great."

But if one member of this same couple understands interviewing techniques or is assisted by a lawyer who understands interviewing techniques, the professional can assist both parties in gaining a great deal more information from such an encounter:

"It's good to be home."

"You look tired, love; was the boss on a rampage again?"

"No. She was reasonable today."

"Sit down in your favorite chair and let me rub your neck."

"That feels nice."

"Your neck is tight. You seem so tense."

"It's Wilson. He can be so difficult at times."

"I know," the spouse replies, continuing the neck rub and demonstrating absolute attention to what is being said.

"Today, he took credit for my design. I had to demand a meeting with the boss to explain the procedure. If she wasn't intelligent and didn't know everything that goes on in the business, Wilson would have been promoted and given a bonus, and I would still be working late at my computer."

"You did the right thing."

"Let me tell you about the design because our future may depend on it. . . ."

The key to drawing out the narrative in this situation is not so much the questions the at-home spouse asks as the sense of genuine interest that his or her tone and attitude convey. Giving the person to be interviewed a comfortable place to sit and eliminating some of the tension (although a connubial neck rub will obviously not be appropriate in every case, especially if a lawyer is involved) are enough to create a calm atmosphere, conducive to letting information out.

Communication between humans is not limited to words: it also includes touch, facial expressions, body position, closeness, and openness. Since before humans came down from the trees to walk upright, touch has been an important part of human interaction. A gentle touch can relax one's partner. A warm and firm handshake can initiate a business meeting and open the parties to full communication.

Even in a marriage where both spouses love, respect, and trust each other, real and enduring communication needs help to develop. By adopting the interviewing technique of absolute, nonconfrontational interest in what the other has to say, no question is required to start the narrative. On the other hand, a short direct question such as "What's bothering you?" can result in a sullen response, with the partner feeling accused or challenged by the implications of the question or its tone. That spouse might respond by withdrawing into a newspaper, not venturing to say anything, or perhaps shifting the topic to "What'll we have for dinner?"

Many married couples *do* know the best way to coax information from each other because they have lived together for many years. But these techniques can still greatly enhance the marriage relationship.

BENEFITS OF SUCCESSFUL INTERVIEWING

Interviewing is an ancient art that has been practiced by human beings since before language was invented. It is an art used whenever two or more human beings meet to share information. People seldom realize that what they are actually doing in any verbal interaction is conducting an interview; most employ some of the techniques described here quite unconsciously.

Information exchange makes for more peaceful relationships. Lawyers often forget that the reason many people seek legal advice is to avoid, rather than engage in, litigation. The person who can artfully use interviewing techniques will be able to keep a relationship loving and happy and avoid litigation.

Certainly, in the context of romance, ignorance is not bliss. On the contrary, a successful interview dissolves ignorance and strengthens interpersonal bonds. Failure to obtain and share information can eventually destroy a relationship, be it business or personal.

If you, as a lawyer, want to be successful in all your relationships, you must eliminate ignorance about every relevant subject of importance.

2

The Art of the Interview

INTERVIEWING IS AN ART FORM

Especially in the context of an informal interview, interviewing is an art: by choosing the right surroundings and the right words, the interviewer creates a situation in which the subject is disarmed and becomes less conscious—even unaware—that he or she is "being interviewed." The appealing environment evoked by the interviewer encourages the subject to provide the information sought.

To accomplish the task and get to the truth, the person gathering information must do as much as possible to make the setting ideal for an interview. When provided with a comfortable environment, the subject will be much more amenable to reveal the needed information. A lawyer's initial witness interviews may be most fruitful if they are conducted away from a formal office environment, with the lawyer sitting behind a desk and the witness in a stiff chair looking up and over the desk to the lawyer. In addition, it is best to hold the interview in a room decorated in warm colors or neutral pastels and furnished with comfortable, "friendly" chairs or sofas.

In a noncriminal context, as often as possible, the professional will conduct the interview in the home of the person interviewed. The professional should take care not to place physical restrictions on the interview setting. The interviewer will never:

- require a man to wear a tie.
- require a woman to wear heels.

- require a desk or other "barrier" to be placed between the participants.
- require a darkened room or harsh lighting.
- require the room temperature to be uncomfortably high or low.

In a manner directly opposite to that of a police interrogation, the interviewer should always have coffee, water, or other beverages available for the person being interviewed. Any chair provided should be a comfortable one. Likewise, the attitude and demeanor of the person gathering the information should always be curious, conciliatory, congenial, and calm.

The interviewer should convince the subject, by both words and appearance, that he or she has an all-consuming desire to gather information. Ideally, the subject should be made to feel the need to quench the interviewer's thirst for knowledge, as if bringing water to a person lost in the desert.

Professionals must do more than just accumulate data, however. A professional uses the interview as a scientist might use an experiment: to observe and classify facts. The chalkboard in Edward Lloyd's coffee shop, for example, would have been useless if the information posted there had not been classified into a format intelligible to his customers—the underwriters who needed the information to decide whether or not to undertake risks on shipments by sea.

Throughout the course of the interview, the professional first takes in information and then collates and classifies it as part of the reporting function after completing the interview. Then the professional can use it to evaluate risk, make a business decision, determine if litigation is appropriate, or otherwise order the processes of life.

The interviewer must remember that the most important aspect of any profession is gathering sufficient information to make an intelligent decision with regard to risk. The mother who wants to know where her child has been is gaining information to make decisions about risks the child faces. The insurance underwriter who asks a prospective insured about the materials used in constructing a building is gathering information to decide whether to accept or reject a risk. The businesswoman who interviews her sales staff is gathering information to decide whether to take a risk on a new product. The manufacturer who interviews his suppliers is gathering information on whether to take a risk on a new manufacturing plant. Finally, the lawyer who interviews a potential client or an independent witness is gathering information on whether to accept the representation of the potential client or whether it is appropriate to file suit on behalf of the potential client.

When it comes to interviewing, experience by itself is not enough. The interviewer must first know the fundamentals and principles that make up the art and science of interviewing. An interviewer needs to understand the techniques of interviewing before starting an interview as much as a surgeon needs to know anatomy before beginning surgery. An untrained person with a scalpel can never perform an adequate appendectomy no matter how often he or she tries. Without a thorough knowledge of anatomy, he or she will not even find the appendix.

Practice without applied knowledge will actually do more harm than good. As the study of anatomy is to the student surgeon, so the fundamentals of the art of the interview are to the lawyer. The professional must first understand the anatomy of the interview.

If the professional does not know the fundamentals and principles of interviewing—and when to apply them—he or she will not advance beyond the level of a novice. Any information gathered will be inadequate, incomplete, and untrustworthy.

Without realizing it, many interviewers are novices at gathering information. If they have even a few random instances of success, they can come to feel they are good interviewers. But it is only through application of the fundamentals and realization of the cause-and-effect relationship of the fundamentals with the resulting information that the professional can truly realize his or her potential as an interviewer.

BEWARE THE "EXPERT" SYSTEM

For centuries, insurers have attempted to make the work of their personnel easy. Insurance agents are provided with blank applications and proposal forms. Lawyers are supplied with lists of questions to ask insureds and claimants. Underwriters are given manuals to help them collate the information they have. More recently, software programs called "expert systems" have been introduced. The software consists of the combined input of a great number of experienced insurance underwriters and professionals in other businesses.

The user merely keys in the facts, and the software makes a decision concerning the suitability of risk and the premiums to be charged, based on the collective input and experience of the underwriters.

The expert systems have a fatal flaw: they assume that the information keyed into the computer is correct. Because the convenience of the new expert systems allows insurers to hire less experienced underwriters, there is a tendency to ask fewer questions. In addition, the underwriter is not "taking risk" as a professional but is merely operating a software program. The use of expert systems, more than data processing, has reduced some aspects of the underwriting profession to nothing.

The lawyer must be aware that the user of an expert system is not even called upon to gather information, let alone to make a decision. In effect, the living, thinking, risk-taking, *human* underwriter has been replaced by a calculator. Information not included in the expert system is simply ignored, to the detriment of the insurer. Neither personal information gathering nor critical judgment is exercised. As a result, successful concealment and misrepresentation by an insured becomes simple, and insurance fraud is encouraged. Judgment is replaced by mechanical calculation, and facts are replaced by uncorroborated digital representations. The insurer's need for an exceptional lawyer with the skill to conduct thorough interviews will provide an ability to eliminate the weaknesses caused by the expert system. On the other hand, the lawyer representing a policyholder who is a skilled interviewer will obtain sufficient evidence to prosecute a claim seeking bad faith tort and punitive damages from an insurer.

Similar expert systems exist in other professions ranging from archaeology to manufacturing and from architecture to zoology. If used at all, expert systems must be used with caution. It is essential that they be augmented with *human* experience, knowledge, and judgment. Personal contact and information gathered by a skillful interviewer are more valuable to the professional than any expert system yet developed. A computer program does not have the ability to mold all the human variables into a useful analysis. A computer program cannot sense the tension in a person's face or the change in body odor when a person begins to tell lies.

How far you advance as a professional interviewer depends on the effort you put into conducting the interview. To become a professional, you must cultivate an insatiable curiosity. Study constantly and experiment with various techniques that may not have been tried before. Most importantly, as a "human expert," listen and never interrupt a narrative.

THE HUMAN EXPERT

To hone interviewing skills, the professional should interview friends and relatives and make a habit of encouraging full responses. The professional listens intently to what each person has to say and can feel the positive effect of such generous and undivided attention: people like to be heard, and they like a person who can listen. Whether practicing or interviewing "for real," the professional never limits the subject to a single topic but instead allows interests and associations to flow unimpeded. As a result, the experienced interviewer is seen as a consummate conversationalist, not as an interrogator.

The interviewer always thinks quickly, having developed a flexibility of mind to fit the changing dynamics of any conversation. This adaptability can convince a subject that the interviewer is genuinely interested in his or her welfare and that it would be advantageous to confide in the interviewer. Our "human expert" knows how to keep his or her emotions, whether empathetic or antagonistic, in check and is always careful not to overextend friendliness such that it could be misread as sympathy or come across as overly serious and thereby convey enmity.

The professional knows that when two individuals are comfortable with each other there is no need to press for information. The professional expects no less than a wealth of details, a satisfying exchange of information, and a successful interview. The professional does not rest until all of the information the witness has is collected and available to the interviewer.

3

General Principles

THE NEED TO TREAT DIFFERENT PEOPLE DIFFERENTLY

No two human beings are alike in how they think and react, any more than two strands of DNA are alike. What induces one person to speak freely can alienate another. Social background is the key determiner. A recent immigrant from a totalitarian regime may be reluctant to give truthful, personal information to anyone in apparent authority for fear of persecution or prosecution. A middle-class teenager raised in the San Fernando Valley of Southern California might enthusiastically and breathlessly relate his entire life story—even if not asked to do so. A person brought up in the Ozarks may feel inclined to go off on a long, apparently unrelated preamble before answering even the simplest question. A lawyer, habitually and masterfully holding her cards close to the chest, will prefer to confine her answers to a minimal "yes" or "no."

Some worldly and sophisticated people are calm and forthcoming in an interviewer's office, while those who are unaccustomed to formal proceedings find the process intimidating and somewhat frightening. Conversely, it sometimes happens that the experienced, sophisticated person will cautiously refuse to communicate in an interviewer's office, while the "average" person will feel perhaps uncharacteristically at ease in the presence of an impressive professional interviewer. And then there is the doctor who will talk freely about medicine but not at all about her real property holdings, or the mechanic who will talk constantly about cars but not say a word about his recreational activities or family life outside of work. In short, no situation—and certainly no person—is ever the same as another.

Similarly, what strikes the conscience of one person interviewed will not evoke the slightest pangs of guilt in another. A person with multiple convictions for perjury probably has an inactive or very sleepy conscience. A person brought up in a Roman Catholic or Jewish family might be more susceptible to techniques that raise feelings of guilt than a confirmed atheist would be. So, for instance, to gain information when interviewing a religious individual, the professional may find it effective to play on the subject's religiously cultivated sense of guilt and his or her probable fear of incarceration or punishment.

The varieties are endless: while one subject will listen and respond cooperatively to reason and logic, another will be more susceptible to an emotion-based appeal. It is up to the interviewer to constantly amend and update the tactics of the interview to fit the personality of the person interviewed.

There is a key to each person interviewed that, when found, will unlock even the most guarded information. By careful and patient questioning, it is the task of the interviewer to find the key and then to exploit it to extract the truth. Once the key is discovered, even the subject may be surprised at how much previously concealed information he or she is ready to reveal.

IT'S HARD TO LIE CONSISTENTLY

The accurately aimed follow-up question is a major tool in the hands of the truly skilled interviewer. No one can lie indefinitely to an experienced, prepared interviewer and get off the hook. On the one hand, when the interviewer is organized, focused, and coherent, the subject is eventually rendered unable to obfuscate or employ avoidance tactics. The subject's efforts to hide lies within irrelevant answers are thwarted because the experienced interviewer does not let such responses stand.

When, on the other hand, an unskilled interviewer bombards the subject with seemingly random and directionless questions, the desired information is almost never gained. The subject sees through the interviewer's lack of questioning technique and soon loses respect for the interviewer's authority.

I once interviewed a person who attempted to answer all my questions with the phrase, "It could be said so." Since "it could be said" that the sun rises in the west, the answers were intended to be as uninformative as possible while still giving the general impression of cooperation. They were, in fact, noncommittal and vague, and less than useless for purposes of the interview. I was eventually able to get relevant information from the person by not succumbing to the ploy. I patiently but persistently repeated and rephrased the questions until the subject replied without qualifying the answer with the evasive and vacuous, "It could be said so."

When the interviewer is organized and well prepared, the subject cannot avoid answering truthfully by using the similar ploy of engaging in "telling stories." Naturally, people convey information in their own personal way, and not in the ideal way an interviewer might envision prior to an interview. A prudent interviewer will therefore encourage narrative responses, careful to wait patiently for the narrative to be completed before moving on to the more specific, more vital, detail required.

Elderly people, for example, often seem to have a need to tell the entire story from beginning to end, rather than recognize and reveal the few essential facts the interviewer requires. With the elderly, practiced patience (and an occasional approving nod of the head) will eventually get the answers needed. Given time, the elderly subject will get to the part of his or her story that is of most relevance to the interviewer. If the professional attempts to break into the narrative, the elderly subject will often stop speaking, look confused, and will either refuse to talk further or begin the same narrative again. When dealing with that type of witness—whether elderly or not—it is essential that the interviewer is patient and allows the full story to play out.

The wise professional listens to an elderly person's entire narrative and, when it is completed, begins the process of honing the information down to the essentials with a series of precise questions that allow for limited, one-word confirmations before proceeding to the next question calling for a new or extended narrative.

Some people, in their desperate attempts to avoid answering questions, can be deliberately devious in their use of the storytelling technique. Take, for example, a subject responding to a simple yes–no question: "Have you ever been insured before this application?"

The nonanswer, in the form of a rambling and convoluted story, might be as follows:

> It was a dark and windy night. My father was away on a business trip, and my mother suggested I get some exercise and stop watching television. I walked to the local bus station whose lunch counter made a great milk shake. My true love came off the bus from Wichita and sat next to me at the lunch counter. His name was Tony Curtis, and we immediately fell in love while sipping our milk shakes, mine chocolate and his strawberry. You see, Tony was an insurance lawyer and traveled a great deal, so. . . .

The question may need to be asked repeatedly—worded differently each time—until it is answered. Each component of the narrative should be broken down, addressed, and clarified with simple, straightforward questions until an unambiguous response is received. Patience, coupled with persistence, is needed to gain all the information available.

One highly useful form of questioning for the lawyer, especially in a trial or deposition setting, is the declarative question, a yes–no question posed in the form of a declarative sentence (i.e., a statement) but spoken with rising intonation at the end. Declarative questions are commonly used in informal speech to express surprise, but their distinctive feature in the context of interviewing is that they ask for verification. The most likely response to a declarative question is agreement or confirmation, but the form is sufficiently open-ended that it allows for detailed, narrative responses as well. It is most effective to narrow responses after the interviewer has listened carefully to narrative responses and needs to obtain limited specific responses.

Regardless of the form the questioning takes, the professional always guides the person interviewed back to the relevant topic and insists on full answers to all the questions asked, even if they must be asked several times. This insistence, however, is always conveyed in a manner suggesting that the interviewer has the proverbial patience of Job. The interviewer, to gain the confidence and cooperation of the interviewee, accepts the blame and may say something like: "I must not have posed my question clearly, John. Let me ask it a different way."

Like a police detective, the interviewer is seeking the truth, but unlike the detective, he or she is also actively and tactically seeking the good faith and trust of the person interviewed. The interviewer cannot compel the subject with the same power of law enforcement that the police have at their disposal. The professional must therefore work even harder to convey the impression that he or she is seeking the information for the sole and noble purpose of providing assistance to the person interviewed. The professional should never say anything to imply that a "wrong" answer to any question could prevent the person interviewed from getting such assistance.

An insurance claims investigator, for example, should make it clear to the insured subject that giving "wrong" answers to questions has no bearing on obtaining insurance or getting a claim paid. Similarly, an employer should never allow an employee to believe that the "wrong" answer might cost the employee a job. The lawyer interviewing a potential client or an independent witness must make clear that there are no possible "wrong" answers to any question posed.

RECOGNIZE INTERNAL INCONSISTENCIES

Despite the fact that as an interviewer you are in a position of dominance over the subject, always be aware that there are no right or wrong answers to the questions posed. The only criteria for the desired answer are that it provide the facts and is true.

When the interviewer has prepared the interview well, the subject intent on lying is forced to create new "facts" to confuse the interviewer. Such creativity usually ends in abject failure. Lies created on the fly invariably include internal contradictions that soon become apparent to the skilled interviewer. Under skilled questioning, the person who has prepared a phony story will either be forced to fabricate further "creative" evasions or, ultimately, to confess to the lie. In contrast, the honest interview subject will be not only truthful but *consistently* truthful. The honest interviewee has no need to create "facts" in an interview and is not limited to the inevitably flawed fiction of a prepared scenario.

The professional is always attuned to the minute details of any narrative elicited and so is able to detect internal inconsistencies or factual contradictions that are the telltale signs of wider prevarication. The interviewer who listens carefully will always discover the falsity of created "facts."

Careful interviewers always check their preparatory notes before concluding the interview. After the interview, they review the recording or transcript, recognizing that some people, by virtue of a pleasant personality or personal charisma, can make the most inane lies seem truthful in a one-on-one situation. By privately reviewing the oral or written record immediately after the conclusion of the interview, interviewers can analyze the information more effectively. Away from the potentially distracting charm of the charismatic subject, the interviewer can more easily spot any weaknesses in the story. A review of the facts in a quiet place, physically removed from the subject, will greatly contribute to the interviewer's exercising his or her powers of reason and help to penetrate the veil of personal charisma.

CREATING ORDER IN THE INTERVIEW

Novice interviewers believe that they can categorize and repeat interviews in the exact same manner and derive precisely the same conclusion, just as a high school science teacher conducts a chemistry experiment. In the laboratory, if two parts of hydrogen are added to one part of oxygen in a closed container and a spark is ignited, water will result. It does not matter how often this experiment is repeated or in what part of the world. If the conditions are consistent, the results will always be the same.

People are innately different from one another. Unlike atoms of hydrogen and oxygen reacting consistently in a laboratory experiment, every person reacts differently to inquiries from a professional interviewer. That is why it is difficult to give procedural rules for conducting an interview: the time, situation, circumstances, and—most importantly—the *people* involved will be different in each case. An experienced interviewer can only apply the general principles that have been formulated and have been found useful in the majority of interview situations and must be flexible enough to change techniques as required by the witness being interviewed.

In every interview, three key variables are at work: the person interviewed, the interviewer, and the topic of the interview. Let's take a closer look at each of these variables.

The Person Interviewed

Every professional recognizes that no two persons interviewed are exactly alike. The person interviewed may even appear to change personality within the course of a single interview. Because the actions of an interviewer can influence the subject's mood and mental outlook, dramatic changes in attitude can be deliberately effected. Five minutes after the interview has started, the interviewer may find that the person he or she has been talking to appears to have taken on an entirely different personality than the one shown at the start of the interview.

For example, a person who is full of anxiety before the interview might relax surprisingly quickly. In fact, subjects often become relaxed once they come to believe, observing an inept interviewer's lack of technique, that they, rather than the interviewer, are controlling the proceedings.

On the other hand, a person who is not particularly worried before the interview starts can quickly come to feel overwhelming tension and anxiety upon the realization that the interviewer is highly competent, well prepared, and in full control of the interview. Once this impression has been made, the subject begins to feel stress, believing that the interviewer has the experience and ability to identify misinformation or expose attempted lies. The person now fears that the interviewer will uncover facts that could establish that he or she is not qualified for a job, is not eligible to receive insurance, was not the victim of a tort, has no viable defense to a suit, or has presented an invalid claim to an insurer. At that point, the person's demeanor and responsiveness may change dramatically.

Professional interviewers are extremely flexible, able to anticipate and act on these changes in the subject. They are able to automatically shift from one tactic to another without obvious intent or belabored thinking. Their techniques merge seamlessly, without any outward indication of a change in tactics. Just as importantly, these interviewers never become so fixed in their ways that they can use only a limited set of techniques; instead, they use whatever technique is most effective at a particular moment, smoothly and with expert timing.

The effective interviewer is continually developing the art of the interview and must always be willing—even as the interview progresses—to create and test new techniques or approaches that feel appropriate and may prove effective. If a particular direction or technique fails, the professional does not draw attention to the miscue but instead moves on quickly and unconcernedly to another approach.

Remember: flexibility in applying techniques is crucial. A technique that works with a man will not necessarily work with a woman; a technique that is effective today may prove totally ineffective tomorrow; and a technique that did not work at all yesterday *will* work today.

The Interviewer

Mood, outlook, and demeanor vary enormously from one interviewer to the next. Some interviewers are more alert and flexible in the morning when they are fresh and relaxed. Others do not become fully alert until noon and cannot be at their best without a hearty breakfast. Still others remain lethargic for hours after a meal. Some are addicted to coffee and cannot seem to function without it, whereas others become hyperactive with just one cup of coffee and lose all ability to be calm and reasonable. An interviewer, near the end of a hard day, will often show the effects of physical fatigue and mental exhaustion just like anyone else. A fatigued interviewer will rush through questions, fail to listen to the answers, and invariably conduct an ineffective interview.

When an interviewer is questioning someone attractive who is making, say, a $1,500 insurance claim, he or she may be emotionally inclined to conduct a gentle interview, using leading questions to elicit information that will allow the client to collect on the claim. In contrast, an interviewer speaking with an unattractive, perhaps dirty or foul-smelling person may have an emotional reaction that makes it difficult to ask simple questions or to get close enough to recognize even clear signs of prevarication.

When interviewing a witness suspected of having started an "arson for profit" fire, the interviewer's emotional reaction to, say, the consequent injury or death of innocent children, may result in an overly aggressive interview. The wise interviewer knows that controlling his or her emotions not only produces the best results but is entirely necessary to achieving a successful interview outcome.

The successful interviewer is detached but simultaneously interested in the person interviewed. The interviewer who allows his or her emotion (rather than reason) to control the interview will fail. The subject will simply return the emotion in kind. Information will not flow unless the interviewer can use the emotions of the person interviewed as a key to opening the locked-in information. It takes self-discipline and willpower for the interviewer to maintain the tone and scope of the interview. A consistent focus on the purpose of the interview and the employment of an evenhanded manner will convince the subject that the professional is dedicated to unlocking the truth.

Granted, there may be situations or moments when a show of emotion is appropriate or even required, but the successful interviewer recognizes that what is primarily involved is a search for the truth, not an occasion for extending sympathy, releasing anger, or exacting revenge. The successful interviewer devotes all the time necessary to get a complete, truthful story and recognizes that, as tiring and emotionally challenging as the process may prove to be, the most important priority is to control the emotions. Interviewers who are unprepared for the emotional rigors of an interview will be unsuccessful, even if they are fully prepared in terms of having researched the subject.

The interview is not an act of verbal free association, nor is it an exercise in emotional anarchy. The interviewer must have a well-defined goal, and that goal must be actively and pointedly pursued. Fortunately, when interviewers are factually prepared and focused on the goal, they will increasingly find that control of emotion becomes somewhat automatic, allowing the interview to more easily move forward to its objective. Once interviewers have their emotions in check, they must recognize the need to take control of the interview and maintain it.

The Interview Topic

It is more difficult to get an inventor to tell the truth about the flaws in his or her technological innovation if the inventor stands to personally profit from the device's popularity and widespread use. Getting the full story from a person who has nothing to gain by promoting the technological advance would be less difficult.

The scale of any investigation is also a factor. It is very difficult to get a person to tell the truth about a major case of arson, whereas the person who has "merely" inflated an insurance claim by saying that burglars stole an HDTV when it was, in fact, a radio, may come around to admitting the truth more easily. In any case, it is always difficult to get interviewees to speak the truth if they stand to personally profit by telling a convincing lie.

The interviewer does not expect—or even aim for—a confession of wrongdoing. Such confessions exist mainly in popular fiction. The subject knows that the interviewer does not have any special powers, especially not the power of the state. The professional has only the relative power of persuasion and the practical skills of a trained interviewer. In the last 52 years of my interviewing experience, only twice have perpetrators actually confessed and admitted to fraud.

Yet the professional knows that it is almost impossible for the subject to keep up a consistent line of falsehoods. The professional also knows that when it becomes clear that a witness is making false statements about facts material to the investigation, that is tantamount to obtaining a confession. Such false statements may allow an insurer (with the advice of counsel or management) to refuse or rescind insurance or to reject a claim. False statements may also allow an employer to refuse to hire a candidate without the risk of a discrimination lawsuit, or they may give the employer sufficient reason to fire an employee. Establishing the falseness of an interview statement made by an industrial designer may prevent a company from manufacturing a dangerous product.

The professional does not become involved in criminal prosecution. If a professional learns that a crime has, in fact, been committed, the law requires the professional to report the crime to the police. However, the professional is not an agent of the police: he or she never makes arrests and never prosecutes crimes. The professional only gathers information and reports facts.

Often the unskillful interviewer chooses, without justification, not to conduct an interview, thinking, “This guy won’t tell us the right time of day . . . he’s a college graduate smart enough to keep his mouth shut,” or, “He has already seen an attorney; he won’t tell me anything useful.” Such a defeatist attitude guarantees that no useful information will ever be gained in an interview. In fact, the more intelligent a person is, or the more he or she has conferred with an attorney, the more the person will be defensive and on guard—and the easier it will be for the professional to uncover the truth. The effective professional uses knowledge about the subject’s education and training to gain rapport. After rapport is established, the person interviewed will be more likely to divulge exactly the information the person had intended to withhold.

BE CONFIDENT—BUT NOT OVERCONFIDENT

Exuding confidence is a major factor in the interviewer’s slow march toward obtaining a successful outcome. When the interviewer conveys a positive attitude, the subject will often pick up on the positive message inferred: telling the truth is the best course of action.

A couple of expressions taken from the world of sport might also be said to apply to interviewing: “A team already defeated before the game begins will be defeated at the end of the game," and "You can't win if you don't show up for the game."

The interviewers who are convinced they will learn nothing are fated to be proven correct. Obviously, an interview that is not conducted produces no information. But it is equally true that an interview conducted without the confident expectation of positive results also produces nothing.

The self-confidence of the interviewer should never overtly control the interview. It should, rather, direct it in a subtle and natural manner. Interviewers should not be so confident of their previously tested ability that the necessary preparation is skimmed over or inadequate. When there is a great deal of physical evidence showing that the subject is presenting a false insurance claim, for example, an interviewer may become overconfident and believe he or she can skip the difficult task of interview preparation. The true professional, though confident of results, is never lulled into this false sense of security.

An overconfident interviewer cannot reason clearly and thus tends not to be reasonable when dealing with the subject. Eventually, experience teaches the overconfident practitioner that such an attitude fails more often than it succeeds.

INTERVIEW CORROBORATION

An inexperienced interviewer tends to believe the most vehement and well-rehearsed denials of wrongdoing, failing to perceive that impassioned protestations of innocence often issue from the guiltiest perpetrators of a particular crime. The professional interviewer understands that the subject may also be a professional—of the criminal kind, that is. The popular image of a guilt-ridden, early-confessing liar comes from the world of television and movies and is largely a fantasy. In reality, the subject who can look the interviewer directly in the eye and smile while blithely spouting lies is encountered much more often than the nervous stereotype eager to give it all up. Almost any defense, when delivered with conviction and confidence, can appear believable.

Think of these famous lies told with conviction:

- "I never had sexual relations with that woman!" (William Jefferson Clinton)
- "I did not know about 'Fast and Furious'." (Eric Holder)

- "The check is in the mail." (every debtor who has ever lived)
- "I have just one more question." (every lawyer who has ever lived)
- "I don't lie." (every liar who has ever lived)

Statements like these can be regarded as partially true and partially false, depending on such factors as intentions, definition of terms, and temporality. The professional never accepts as sufficient such overly simplified statements posing as all-encompassing facts. They require further questioning, corroboration if possible, and much more detail. Bill Clinton's lie was believable until the blue dress appeared. The lawyer's lie becomes obvious when he or she asks a second question.

It is the professional's job to pierce the simplistic or ambiguous statement to find the truth. He or she does so by insisting on finer detail. When the thorough interview is completed, the interviewer will have uncovered the elaborate truth that these sly, vague utterances attempt to conceal.

The interviewer poses the ultimate question of guilt not to gain a confession so much as to facilitate some insight into the personality of the person interviewed.

BODY LANGUAGE

Involuntary and unconsciously performed body movement that communicates information about the subject is commonly called body language. When a subject is asked a question about a presumably falsified Harvard degree, he or she gives the interviewer a great deal of information in the form of twitches, blinks, and/or monosyllabic responses. Every movement, every shift of seating position, every scratch, shrug, or detectable change in body odor, is noted by the professional interviewer and measured in relation to the question asked.

The professional interviewer should always watch the subject and should therefore never write or review notes during the actual interview. The reason is that in taking notes, it is difficult to maintain both eye contact and careful observation of all potentially revealing body language. To facilitate the ability to view the witness, a second person should be available to take notes and operate an audio or video recorder as the interview proceeds, so that the interview can be guided by the body language of the witness.

The professional always seeks the best position for observing the subject—by sight, smell, and touch. If possible, the thorough interviewer positions him- or herself in close proximity to the person being interviewed. Often, how a subject answers a question—more than the subject's actual words—is most informative to the professional. Touch, such as a hand on a shoulder to sitting so close the knees touch, though seldom used by interviewers, can be used to create a sense of intimacy and provide an opportunity to evaluate muscle tension in the witness. When the subject tenses any area of the body such as the brow, mouth, pectoral muscles, legs, or back, the attentive interviewer may interpret this change as an indication that the subject is not being totally truthful. A subject intent on telling the truth will (figuratively and sometimes quite literally) reach out to touch the interviewer. The proximity of the interviewer, the feeling of strength and confidence conveyed, and the ease of casual and friendly touch, can give the subject a sense of trust that will assist in the entire evaluation.

The professional must attune four of the senses—hearing, sight, touch, and smell—to the person being interviewed in order to properly evaluate the information provided. Often, in making this evaluation, a second interviewer may prove useful, observing the subject's gestures while the principal interviewer asks questions. The second interviewer may also take detailed notes while the first concentrates on the physical clues presented by the witness.

The sense of smell in particular can help the interviewer uncover the truth. A person who is being dishonest will frequently exude an odor different from that of a person in a calm state who has no reason to lie. The experienced interviewer will move close enough to the witness to detect and learn to recognize changes in odor, and may even be in a position to notice a change in the witness's sense of taste; an anxious witness who gets dry mouth may be unable to taste the difference between coffee and water or another beverage.

Body language is a rich source of clues for the professional, but an overly developed aesthetic sense—especially an appreciation of physical attractiveness—may work against the interviewer. The good looks of a subject should have no more effect on the interviewer than the bland features of another. The lack of personal hygiene in one subject should be regarded with the same detachment as another's youthful peaches-and-cream complexion. Similarly, a socialite's articulate manner should have no more effect on the interviewer than the crude, uneducated language of a rube. The professional, in focusing on the task at hand, must develop a neutral attitude with regard to essentially irrelevant aesthetic features: those of beauty or homeliness, schooled sophistication, or uneducated boorishness.

CONTROL OF THE INTERVIEW

The role of the interviewer also involves maintaining constant control of the situation, as detailed in Chapter 7. The professional, however, never resorts to bullying the person interviewed. The ability to remain alert and to focus his or her attention, coupled with a facility for nimble thinking, enables the interviewer to direct the questions exclusively at the specific objectives of the interview, while not in any way limiting the subject's willingness to offer a fuller narrative.

Some subjects will attempt to distract the interviewer from his or her mission. For example, they may try to deflect difficult, pointed questions by falling into long narratives containing many irrelevancies. The prudent interviewer will listen carefully to even these long off-topic narratives, since they may provide many new useful lines of questioning. The interviewer knows that rambling, drawn-out, divergent narratives will ultimately lead to follow-up questions and inquiries into areas that the person interviewed intended to avoid. A person who, for purposes of adding credibility, attempts to distract the interviewer in this off-the-cuff manner will necessarily include much truthful information within the narrative.

The professional knows how difficult it is for any subject to create, on the spot, a fully fleshed-out lie. With practiced patience and professional attention to detail, the truth can eventually be revealed. If, however, these common avoidance tactics succeed in distracting the interviewer, the result will be loss of control of the process to the person interviewed. A distracted interviewer will pursue the irrelevant and gain little information; a skilled interviewer will note and absorb narrative sidetracks but always retain control by returning the subject to the relevant points.

The interviewer, though in midprocess, always remains focused on the objectives of the interview. No amount of obfuscation will move the skilled interviewer from those objectives; no amount of deflection will sway him or her from returning to them; and no number of long, irrelevant narratives and sidetracks will exhaust the interviewer's determination to achieve them.

DISCLOSE AS LITTLE INFORMATION AS POSSIBLE

In order to maintain control of the direction and flow of the interview, the interviewer is also careful not to give away information that may tip the balance of power in favor of the person interviewed. This is particularly true when the subject uses the most common ploy of nonresponse. Rather than offering up information to the witness in an effort to make the witness talk, the interviewer calmly, but determinedly, repeats and rephrases unanswered questions. Once it becomes clear that the ploy of uncooperativeness will not serve to frustrate or distract the interviewer, the answers will quickly become more succinct, to the point, and truthful.

Similarly, professional interviewers should never expect a subject to reciprocate automatically when the interviewer offers information. A well-prepared interviewer, in possession of established and substantiated facts gained through prior investigation, will often begin by asking only questions whose answers are already known. If the person interviewed answers with the same information that the interviewer knows to be true, the facts are therefore additionally corroborated by the subject, and the interviewer establishes that—at least in these instances—the subject is telling the truth. If the subject's answers diverge from the facts, then prevarication is clearly established.

It is not the interviewer's job to inform the subject of any gathered facts whatsoever. The interviewer should restrict comments about preinterview knowledge to generalities and instead must elicit as much information as possible while revealing as little as possible. Understandably, the person being interviewed will ask about the investigation. The response should be succinct and polite, providing only as much information as courtesy requires. In fact, subjects who notice that the interviewer offers up information too easily will lose respect for the interviewer and so will often provide even less information.

Any person interviewed will only give information when convinced that the interviewer is a professional and worthy of respect. (This is even more the case when the person interviewed is trying to hide something.)

In fact, if the interviewer is polite but reticent, the subject is more likely to believe that the interviewer already has enough information and that lies will not work.

At the same time, the interviewer should avoid any show of professed ignorance. While it is true that such admissions can occasionally cause subjects to let down their guard, more often they cause subjects to lose respect for the interviewer. In addition, subjects must feel that the interviewer is intelligent and that they are naturally expected to be forthcoming with truthful information. In short, the interviewer must walk a fine line between appearing ignorant and appearing merely "*incompletely* informed" of the facts.

Leading questions are also a dangerous tactic and therefore unwise. The experienced interviewer avoids using such questions because they always reveal to the subject too much of what the interviewer knows. More importantly, leading questions direct the subject toward "expected" or predetermined responses rather than working to reveal the truth.

One more point should be made regarding the importance of controlling an interview: a sophisticated subject may be as knowledgeable about these interview approaches and techniques as the interviewer is. Professionals are, therefore, always on guard to identify whether that the subject is using such techniques against them.

EXPLOIT THE SUBJECT'S NEED TO BE FLATTERED

It is natural to want to show one's degree of intelligence or depth of expertise. The experienced interviewer uses this universal aspect of human nature to gain information. The successful interviewer demonstrates an insatiable curiosity for everything the person interviewed knows and shows an uncommon interest in everything the interviewee says. The subject, now flattered, becomes more cooperative in an attempt to satisfy the interviewer's curiosity.

Conveying a sense of curiosity is not sufficient, though. The interviewer must follow up with genuine, attentive listening. Interviews often fail when the interviewer simply does not listen to what is being said. If, for example, the interviewer is concentrating on the next question rather than truly listening to the subject, vague or misdirected answers will never be clarified. Useful information that would have benefited from a follow-up question will not be noticed or recognized as important. The interview will develop gaps and will be incomplete.

An interview is a living, self-articulating interchange that the interviewer needs to help keep alive. Each answer the interviewer receives leads naturally (and often but not always logically) to the next question. If the interviewer fails to listen carefully to the answers, the branching pattern that characterizes a skillfully conducted interview will not arise. The interviewer's questions will sound as if they are coming from a prepared list, and so they will be ineffective. Although effective preparation for an interview may indeed include compiling a list of questions to be asked in syllogistic order, listening carefully to the answers presented by the witness requires leaving the prepared list behind and using it only at the end to make sure all subjects have been covered.

The flexible interviewer strives to remember questions that have not been fully answered and comes back to them later. Questions can be "repeated" by changing the context or by paraphrasing them.

CONTROLLING THE INTERVIEW: A SUMMARY

The interviewer keeps control of the interview by:

- being prepared for every eventuality.
- listening carefully to the answers given.
- taking cues from the demeanor of the interviewee.
- never being distracted by irrelevancies.
- projecting the image of a person who is genuinely curious and interested.
- refusing, politely but firmly, to accept a nonresponsive attitude.
- using multiple types of questioning tactics so as not be repetitious or annoying.

In a nutshell, the professional interviewer must have the proverbial patience of Job, the legendary wisdom of King Solomon, the dynamic confidence of James Bond, and the kind demeanor and conversational skills of Oprah.

4

The Interviewer

THE NEED TO LEARN CONTINUALLY

Interviewing resembles a science in just one way: it is concerned with the observation and classification of facts. The interview affords a person a method for becoming intelligently informed on any subject. At its heart, though, it is an art.

Interviewers study people, not immutable laws of nature. As we saw in Chapter 3, because no two people are the same, the interview can never be subject to scientific rules the way the study of chemistry or physics is. Nonetheless, a quasi-scientific approach can help interviewers refine their skills, provided they carefully document and review the interviews they conduct.

The proverb, "The more I learn, the more I know how little I know," applies to the study of the interview as much as to that of any science, art, or philosophy. No person, in any profession or sport, nor at whatever level of skill, ever becomes so proficient that he or she cannot improve. The best athletic teams look upon an actual game as a form of practice. By reviewing video footage, gleaning information from scouting reports, and actively pursuing detailed knowledge, players and coaches learn what their weaknesses are, and they come to understand where and why they have failed in the past. Constantly building on this knowledge base, they improve.

With this point in mind, soon after completing each interview—whether successful or not—interviewers should review it in detail, with an eye to learning to conduct the next one even better. In those cases where interviewers have obtained exceptional results, they will want to identify the moments at which the subject was most forthcoming (and note the techniques that had such an effect). The professional also analyzes any weaknesses in any interview, especially in those investigations that yielded only minimal information.

If a colleague has listened to the interview, the interviewer can learn by asking the colleague for feedback. Such objective third parties can reveal which techniques were effective and which did not work.

Professionals never fail to seek advice on technique from other professionals and colleagues. Interviewers who are willing to listen objectively to such advice may discover that they did not follow up openings or apply listening skills, or that they unwittingly brought the process to an untimely halt before obtaining the answer sought.

If a tape or digital recorder was used in the interview, interviewers should play the recording back and analyze it objectively as if a colleague had conducted the interview. Delaying review for at least a week, if possible, will bolster objectivity.

As the need for reviewing cases shows, interviewers must always be trying to improve their skills. The interviewer, and every lawyer, perpetually remain students, always learning and always working to improve with each new interview.

THE POWER OF OBSERVATION

The entire conclusion of an interview is based on an accumulation of observations the interviewer makes regarding the witness. The importance of learning from observation is not new. Think of George Bernard Shaw's words: "If you leave the smallest corner of your head vacant for a moment, other people's opinions will rush in from all quarters." In order to maintain perspective, interviewers must not let other people's opinions—including those of the person interviewed—colonize their minds.

Consider what Shakespeare had Julius Caesar say: "I do not know the man I should avoid / So soon as that spare Cassius. He reads much. / He is a great observer, and he looks / Quite through the deeds of men. . . . / Such men as he . . . are they very dangerous. . . ."

To read, in Shakespeare's usage, is to observe, and here Cassius, like an interviewer, "reads much." The interviewer, now as then, must be a great observer. The professional must look through concealments to see the actual deeds of people. The professional is a potent threat to those attempting to hide information. The criminal, the liar, the embezzler, all have much to fear from an interviewer who emulates the Cassius that Caesar feared. In the presence of a demonstrably observant interviewer, a subject with something to hide cannot maintain a poker face, let alone sustain deception and lies.

A CAVEAT

Often the wary subject can read the interviewer's intentions, thoughts, and emotions from tone of voice, posture, body position, and facial expressions better than the less skilled interviewer can note the subject's outward signs of emotion and evident thought patterns. To convey to the subject the understanding that the interview is a process of advocacy for truth, interviewers must know how to project what appear to be genuine feelings of helpfulness, friendliness, and empathy. If interviewers cannot do this, they should take acting lessons, join a community theater, or read books on how to perform.

THE ACTOR'S CRAFT

How a person initially feels toward a stranger is often completely dependent on the stranger's facial expressions and body language. If the stranger's expression projects anger or hatred, most people tend to feel it and to reflect the emotion in kind. If posture or body language suggests resistance or distrust, that feeling, too, is unconsciously reflected back at the viewer.

If, however, the professional knows how to "act" and uses positive facial expressions and body language that convey confidence, trustworthiness, and kindness, the subject will feel much more inclined to return the favor. Creating such an atmosphere through simple but convincing acting techniques goes a long way toward enabling interviewers to access the information they need.

The professional knows how to communicate a calm demeanor, an aura that seems to emanate from a state of inner peace. The subject, feeling this disposition, interprets it as goodwill and friendliness. The professional who can set up the emotional sphere of the interview and positively influence the subject in this manner will achieve better results than the professional who is not schooled in such essential acting skills.

It would be useful to the lawyer, acting as an interviewer or cross-examiner, to study the techniques actors use to convey emotions. Classes in improvisational acting typically present actors with a personality and fact situation and ask them to improvise a conversation. When the United States Army Intelligence school trained me as a interviewer, it hired professional actors to be witnesses who would submit to an interview but would only provide the information properly presented. They would be emotional, angry, quiet, subtle, or frightened as the subject matter required. This great learning tool should be part of every law school curriculum.

PREJUDICE BLOCKS THE TRUTH

The foremost aim of the interview is to learn the truth, the whole truth, and nothing but the truth. Truth can only be obtained by accurately classifying facts obtained through a methodical and detailed investigation and interview. In this regard, the greatest danger any interviewer faces is that resulting from entering into an interview with preconceived opinions.

As the philosopher and psychologist William James said, "A great many people think they are thinking when they are merely rearranging their prejudices."

No professional can conduct an effective interview if he or she is convinced, prior to the start of the interview, that the witness will be truthful (or untruthful). The professional must remain vigilant in this regard, avoiding all preconceived opinions and prejudices that could endanger the success of an interview.

Sometimes an unskilled interviewer will jump to a conclusion of guilt long before the interview itself is conducted. Based on such information as the subject's family background, social position, or seeming lack of an alibi, the novice interviewer's tendency to prejudge will inevitably limit the effectiveness of the truth-seeking process and the scope of the interview. Starting an interview with a preconceived notion of any kind will simply cause the interviewer to miss important facts: facts that his or her prejudices did not envision or investigate.

The tendency to prejudge is extremely common. Insurance brokers, being consummate salespeople, feel that a wealthy customer who pays the full premium before inception could never deceive them. Mothers ardently believe their children would never lie to them. Most police officers cannot comprehend that a wealthy individual living in Beverly Hills or Vail could ever commit a petty crime. Judges and lawyers doubt children have the guile to effectively lie to them. Most businesspeople believe a long-time or politically connected customer would never cheat.

Similarly, many inexperienced interviewers immediately assume that an individual is lying because the individual has a past criminal record or belongs to a particular racial group or religion, or for any other of the many "reasons" founded in the interviewer's own personal bias. Every professional must avoid prejudice based on preconceptions about the subject's wealth, age, gender, race, religion, or national origin, not simply as an obvious and positive egalitarian principle, but as anathema to conducting a successful interview. Everyone has prejudices, but the prudent professional recognizes this fact, places judgment "on hold," and keeps it out of any interview.

When conducting an interview, professionals accept that a witness will also, paraphrasing William James's words, be "rearranging his or her prejudices" throughout the process. Interviewers who cannot dismiss bias during an interview tend to look for and listen to only those things that confirm their prejudice. Such interviewers will never obtain the truth. And even if the truth does present itself, they will not hear it if it does not comport with the preconceptions, biases, and prejudices they bring to the interview.

THE INTERVIEWER WHO IS NOT OBJECTIVE HAS FAILED BEFORE THE INTERVIEW BEGINS

To avoid the negative effects of his or her own prejudices, the professional:

- believes only what is corroborated and proven.
- never lets personal biases or prejudices color his or her judgment.
- never allows a subject's personal charisma to influence or curtail an interview.
- exploits the expressed prejudices of the subject to gain truthful answers.

Yes, you read that last point right: ironically, the skilled interviewer can use a witness's prejudices and preconceived notions to get to the truth more quickly. For example, when interviewing a person who expresses racist opinions, the interviewer can use knowledge of those prejudices to develop a false but effective rapport with the subject. Or by challenging the subject's apparent racist attitudes, the interviewer can anger the subject enough that the subject lets loose with a vituperative explosion of words that could provide the breakthrough needed to allow the interviewer to get the whole truth.

DEMEANOR OF THE INTERVIEWER: ALWAYS REMAIN CALM

Never lose your temper. It's liable to frighten the subject, and few will respond to or confide in those whom they fear. Faced with rage, subjects will limit their answers to single-syllable words and provide no useful information.

Furthermore, interviewers who lose their temper will no longer be able to think clearly or plan the next step in the interview. They will be forced to cede control of the interview, which will render it ineffective. Like a chess match, the interview must be planned and executed with knowledge of the next 4 to 10 moves; there is no room for outbursts of temper. If the interviewer lacks anger management skills, the interview is bound to fail.

MAINTAIN PERSPECTIVE

The professional never lets a subject think that a full response to all questions is more important to the professional than it is beneficial to the witness him- or herself. Therefore, the professional should not appear to be trying too hard and should not permit his or her consciousness of the interview's importance to contribute to an atmosphere of stress. Much as the manager of a business might tell his or her sales personnel not to use the hard-sell technique on a client, the skilled interviewer should not appear to be trying too hard to "oversell" the witness on the necessity of telling the truth. Rather, the interviewer should convey confidence that the truth will be forthcoming.

The interviewer who tries too hard to convince the witness of the necessity for telling the truth is like the young Roman Catholic girl who fell in love with a Protestant. Her mother suggested that perhaps he could be taught the tenets of their faith and be converted to Roman Catholicism. A week after religious instructions began, the girl came home in tears. She sobbed: "I oversold him! He's decided to study for the priesthood!"

HAVE FAITH IN YOUR ABILITIES AND IN THE PROCESS

An interviewer will on occasion be discouraged by the lack of progress in an interview. It is important to keep in mind that these periods of depression are also experienced by the world's greatest athletes, singers, and other performers.

One of two things can happen to the interviewer facing an interview slump:

- The interviewer becomes so discouraged that he or she gives up trying.
- The interviewer works his or her way out of the situation.

Far from succumbing, the professional persists by resorting to multiple tried-and-true techniques, sticking to the fundamentals, and maintaining confidence in the process until the truth is obtained. Like a baseball player in a hitting slump, the professional recognizes that it is necessary to work through the slump—to continue confidently applying the process until success ensues. The professional who keeps studying, practicing, reviewing, and interviewing will find that such periodic slumps soon come to an end. He or she recognizes that instances of failure are just slip-ups on the stepping stones on the path to becoming a truly great interviewer.

THE EFFECTIVE INTERVIEWER

The effective interviewer:

- has self-confidence and demonstrates it.
- is courteous, even in the face of discourtesy.
- honors his or her promises and controls his or her passions.
- wins respect by being respectful and respectable.

- turns up with a smile even when turned down.
- understands and is understood by people.
- has faith in purpose.
- is persistent.
- gets all the truth that can be gotten from an interview.

QUALIFICATIONS OF AN INTERVIEWER

A skilled interviewer's key qualities include:

- an interest in the operations of human nature.
- a thorough knowledge of the principles of civil investigation.
- a thorough knowledge of the specific subject matter of the interview.
- the ability to engender trust and inspire confidence.

Actors often have months in which to learn their lines, practice their gestures, and incorporate their reactions. Moreover, movie or TV actors can always call for a retake if anything goes wrong in a performance. The great actor can affect our emotions, even though we know the lines the actor speaks are only those scripted by professional writers. We cry at the death scene, even as we are fully aware that it is just the movie character who is dying, and not the actor, whose sixth divorce was splashed all over the tabloids the week before.

Must the interviewer be an actor? The answer is decidedly no! He or she must be more than just an actor: the true interview professional must be a consummate actor, the kind of acting professional who does not merely mouth lines someone else has had the luxury of many weeks' time to write. The interviewer must be ready to improvise and deliver lines with lightning speed, adapting to any and all possible shifts in the interview drama. He or she has no meaningful chance to practice the art of the interview except *within* the interview itself. Neither is the interviewer provided with a director who will demonstrate the use of gestures to maximize dramatic effect. The interviewer is strictly and entirely alone. Any mistakes made in the interview are final. There are no retakes.

An ordinary stage actor performs in front of an audience that is at least 20 feet away, whereas the audience members to whom the professional interviewer plays can be as close as 4 inches away. If the performance is less than flawless, the audience will not believe the performance and will be silent. If the audience is silent, the performance—the interview—is a failure.

When an actor is doing a good job, the performance itself is invisible. The audience suspends disbelief and the character being portrayed comes to life. Similarly, although the witness recognizes when the interviewer is doing a bad job, a good performance by the actor/interviewer passes for reality and the subject becomes convinced of the interviewer's persona and role, forgetting for the moment—or never fully realizing—that he or she is being interviewed. When the interviewer's acting skills are "on," the interviewer and the subject become just two interested parties having a lively conversation. Information gained from that purposeful but improvised "conversation" is more detailed than any information extracted through the well-known "third degree" tactic of interrogation. The subject will have no hesitation to converse and will freely convey information.

Consummate acting skills, along with patience and diligence, will give the interviewer information-laden answers such as:

"I obtained my Master's degree in biology from Oxford."

"I'd never wear those ugly-ass shoes!"

"It depends on what the meaning of 'is' is."

"She had sex with me. I did not have sex with her."

"I didn't buy any gasoline in a can."

"I never had an insurance policy canceled."

All these answers are definite statements that can be corroborated, supported, or proven false by further investigation. If lies are produced in the free flow of this well-acted conversation, they can eventually be proven to be such. If the truth emerges, the ongoing interview and continuing investigation will corroborate it. In either case, the interviewer's acting skill will have produced a wealth of material that can be verified later, and the interview will be well on the way to a successful conclusion.

The person interviewed is the toughest drama critic in the world. If the interviewer does the acting job correctly, the subject will become not only a spectator but also a willing participant, and a complete story will unfold. The subject who participates and tells a complete story even when doing so disadvantages him or her is in effect giving the interviewer a rave review! Again, the acting can only be of the highest quality: if the understudy actor/novice interviewer hams it up or flubs a line, the subject will immediately sense the attempted deception and withdraw. The interview will effectively be over. No matter how long the "performance" is dragged out, it will get nowhere.

THE INTERVIEW IS A SALES PRESENTATION

The interviewer should be both a great actor and a better-than-great salesperson. No doubt, everyone has bought products from charming and effective salespersons, even when we didn't want an article or felt it was overpriced. We still bought the item because the salesperson's skill convinced us that we couldn't do without it. The worst thing that can happen when a skilled salesperson's pitch is accepted is that a little money gets spent.

In an interview situation, however, the subject might stand to lose the ability to be insured, a lawsuit may be lost, a contract may not be signed, a job or promotion may be lost or won. The proceeds of an insurance claim may be at risk, or the ability to prove a tort may be lost. In extreme but not uncommon cases, the person who is asked to "tell the whole truth" may even face criminal prosecution. Everything from personal security to social standing may be in jeopardy, and carefully phrased and guarded responses meet every inquiry from the interviewer.

What many great salesmen have found true should be of extreme interest to professional interviewers.

SALESMANSHIP FOR THE PROFESSIONAL INTERVIEWER

Here are the basic rules of salesmanship as they apply to the professional interviewer.

Sell Yourself Thoroughly on Your Product

To sell the interviewer's product, which is honesty, integrity, and a desire for complete and truthful information, the interviewer must be convinced that what he or she has to sell is exactly what the subject needs or wants. Once the professional is sold on the product, he or she can more easily get the person interviewed to adopt a similar attitude.

An agreement about the purpose and benefits of finding the truth means that the person interviewed will be much more inclined to tell a complete story—to "buy into" the interviewer's goals. The subject knows what the interviewer wants—the truth—and is sold on the importance of telling all to the professional.

Like the Customer

People relate more favorably to those who seem to like them than to those who do not. For example, in a restaurant, a waiter might walk up to a customer and say, "Well, what do you want, Fatso?"

The customer might react by demanding to speak with the manager, telling the waiter off and punching him in the nose, or simply leaving, never to return. It is unreasonable to think that a customer, being exposed to such abuse, would be willing to stay there and calmly order a meal. No matter how hungry the customer might be, another restaurant will surely get the business.

The same is true of an interview. The subject who senses antagonism from the interviewer will almost always choose not to be a consumer of what the interviewer is trying to sell. The subject/customer may sit at the table but will not partake of the meal. However, if the interviewer makes an honest effort to like the subject, the person interviewed will order multiple courses. A cultivated affinity for the subject will draw out more information than ants attracted to a picnic blanket.

Establish Rapport

No matter how despicable a person is, the professional always endeavors to find something to admire or respect in that individual. The professional learns how to develop empathy for, and interest in, the person interviewed. The interviewer should select and focus on one trait of the subject that is genuinely admirable and that the interviewer shares with the subject. The interviewer's display of empathy can be convincing, for example, if the interviewer makes clear that the two of them share such things as:

- a similar family background.
- faith or membership in the same religious denomination.
- a record of distinguished military service.

- children of the same age.
- club affiliation.
- a hobby or an interest.

During the interview, the professional should occasionally refer to, or casually elaborate on, the single key feature he or she shares with or admires in the subject. This tactic will put the subject at ease.

If, however, an interview starts with the unskilled interviewer making overt attempts to establish superiority, express contempt, or even resort to name-calling and swearing, common sense tells us that the subject will not give the interviewer any relevant information.

Rapport with the person interviewed is the key to a successful interview. Until the interviewer establishes rapport with the person interviewed, the interview is more like a duel of wits—a duel with heavy sabers. It is exhausting and unproductive for both involved. Once the professional establishes rapport, the interview is transformed into the equivalent of a conversation between neighbors over a backyard fence.

The interviewer cannot cheat or lie to establish rapport; he or she must find an area of genuine mutual interest or attributes. Common ground between any two individuals can be found with a modicum of effort, as is also discussed in Chapter 1.

Rapport is the first step in changing the subject's emotional status. Once rapport is established, the interview becomes a joint enterprise rather than a battle of wits.

Compliment the "Customer"

If you cannot find any significant points you have in common with the subject, give honest compliments such as:

> "You have a unique hairstyle. Can I have the phone number of your hairdresser?"
>
> "Your home is comfortable."
>
> "Your office looks so efficient."
>
> "You have a well-behaved collie."
>
> "Your children are lovely."

Use of such compliments must "come from the heart"; otherwise the subject will suspect the interviewer of employing transparent flattery.

A clothing store clerk may use one approach to sell to a stout man, "Oh, that suit makes you look very slim." The same salesman, wishing to sell the same style suit, will tell a thin man, "Oh, that suit brings out your fine physique." No successful salesman would use the following sales pitch: "Wow! You look like a grey flannel Michelin Man in that suit. Say, have you ever thought of knocking off about 50 pounds of that fat? How do you get into the shower?"

This insulting manner would never sell a suit. But many unskilled interviewers, who unwittingly or consciously insult their subjects, are simply unaware that insults are entirely counterproductive.

Although it may be difficult, the interviewer should attempt to be as politically neutral as possible with each interview. The true professional never tries to ingratiate him- or herself to the witness by making derogatory remarks concerning sensitive topics such as race, religion, politics, or sexual orientation. Such unenlightened attempts at negative bonding with the subject will as often as not result in the subject feeling insulted.

Once insulted in this way, the subject will lose all respect for the interviewer and will not answer any questions. Unskilled interviewers, in an attempt to create a bond with the subject by telling a story that makes fun of others, will find that their lack of cultural sensitivity or restraint destroys the interview process.

This type of interviewer did not learn the truth of the old proverb that "You catch more flies with honey than with vinegar." Good manners and honest curiosity always lead to more information than bluster and false camaraderie. When interviewers, rather than denigrating a social group, compliment the subject/customer in a sincere manner, they are often rewarded with information. The person interviewed who feels liked by the interviewer will meet courtesy in kind and cooperatively volunteer all the information required.

Indeed, the comical expression "Flattery will get you everywhere" is a truism that the professional knows well and will always apply judiciously.

Cultivate the Right Attitude

Every fall weekend, any number of low-ranking football teams, be they college or pro, upset superior teams. Every spring day, many inferior baseball teams win games against teams with superior rosters. Position for position, the winning team members have less skill and strength than their opponents. Yet they can, and often do, win. Why? The reason is simple: they have the will to win.

A superior mental attitude in less talented players causes them to do a superior job. The same effect applies to interviewers. Interviewers must cultivate a positive state of mind that will make them look forward eagerly to starting the interview and make them hunger for success. The interviewer establishes the proper state of mind and conveys the resulting positive attitude, whether he or she is a news reporter, a civil attorney, or any other person needing information from another person.

SELL YOURSELF FIRST

Once the professional has adopted the proper mental attitude, he or she begins by selling the subject on his or her personality. As a result, the subject now perceives that the professional is doing "a good deed" in conducting the interview. It is almost impossible for the average person to resist a confident, direct, and purposeful interviewer.

Influenced by the professional's personality, the subject realizes that the interviewer can be most useful, gaining a number of things, for instance:

- career advancement;
- the desired insurance;
- proof of claim to the insurer;
- payment of other monies;
- status in the corporation;
- a cure for illness; or
- 15 minutes of fame on the local TV news.

The professional must be convinced that society as a whole will be better off if a thorough interview is completed. He or she must feel that it is to the general advantage that a voluntary, trustworthy, and complete statement be secured. Then, and only then, can the professional begin to instill the same attitudes in the subject.

When the subject has endorsed the interviewer's agenda and shares the goal of finding the truth, the real "talk" can begin. In a well-prepared interview, the questions and answers will come easily. Getting the whole truth requires the skill of an experienced interviewer, one who can gain the trust of the person interviewed, making the case that all that is required of the person is truth. With skill and perseverance, the interviewer convinces the interviewee that telling the whole truth is in his or her best interest.

SIX KEY INTERVIEW QUESTIONS

The objective of every interview is to determine the answer to six questions:

- Who?
- What?
- When?
- Where?
- Why?
- How?

When these key questions are answered, the professional will know all that is necessary to decide to insure or not to insure; to present a risk to one underwriter or to another; to agree or decline to pay a claim; to manufacture one product and not another; to hire one employment candidate or the other; or to start a business or not. The interview can only be a success after all six questions are answered fully.

The questions are universal, and they form the outline for every interview. The information needed to make any decision in *any* interview situation rests on the answers to these questions.

When preparing for an investigative interview (see Chapter 5 for a discussion of preparation), the following list provides examples and variants as they might be posed in the variety of interview situations noted above.

Who?

- Who is the person interviewed?
- Who is the claimant?
- Who is our customer?

- Who is our competitor?
- Who is necessary to the success of our business?
- Who did what to whom?
- Who has something to gain?
- Who has an interest in the outcome of the investigation?
- Who has something to lose from the investigation?
- Who are independent witnesses?
- Who knows any of the facts in question?
- Who might have information about the facts in question?
- Who did it?
- Who will know in the future where you live or how to contact you?

What?

- What is required to produce our product?
- What is insured?
- What risk is the applicant seeking to insure?
- What caused the person to seek insurance?
- What happened to cause a loss?
- What is our product?
- What makes a profit?
- What is the cost of the investigation?
- What are the names of every person interviewed?
- What did the subject do?
- What does the subject know?
- What does the subject want from the professional?
- What does the professional want to accomplish by the investigation?
- What is the price of the product?
- What is the subject's connection to the inquiry?
- What is the amount of the claim?
- What is the value of the property claimed stolen?
- What is the net worth of the person interviewed?
- What is the subject's address and telephone number?

Where?

- Where did the incident happen?
- Where is the evidence?
- Where is the prospective insured?
- Where is the property the insured seeks to insure?
- Where is the loss?
- Where is the risk?
- Where are the people who will buy our product?
- Where are the raw materials needed to make our product?
- Where are the people who can build our product?
- Where was the subject located at the time of the incident?
- Where are the records that support the position of the subject?

When?

- When is the best time to sell the product?
- When is the insurance needed?
- When is the application made?
- When did the loss occur?
- When will the raw materials be available?
- When can the needed personnel be in place?
- When did the subject observe the incidents under investigation?
- When did the topic of the interview occur?

Why?

- Why is the investigation being conducted?
- Why was the professional asked to obtain information?
- Why do we need to hire this person?
- Why is insurance being sought?
- Why did the insured go to a specific broker?
- Why did the loss occur?
- Why do we need to sell this product?

- Why can this product help us make a profit?
- Why was the subject at the scene of the incident?
- Why does the subject want to talk to the professional?
- Why does the subject want to avoid talking to the professional?

How?

- How did the incident occur?
- How do we protect against our competitors?
- How much did the product cost?
- How do we build the product?
- How do we make money?
- How did the subject become involved in the incident?

No human resources director should think his or her work is complete until the prospective employee has answered all six questions. No chairperson should be satisfied until all six questions are answered by the board and the officers. No doctor should be satisfied that the history provided by his patient is complete until the patient has answered all of the six questions. No lawyer should be satisfied that the information provided by her client accurately answers all six questions.

There is no better way to ensure the quality of the investigative package than with clear, detailed interviews. The organizations whose professionals are good interviewers will save a great deal of money, as well as time and effort.

No professional can claim the title "interviewer" until mastering this most productive of all investigative techniques—obtaining complete answers to the "who, what, where, when, why, and how" questions.

OTHER WAYS OF GETTING ANSWERS

The best way to learn the answers to the six key questions is to obtain the answers from the persons involved. The insured, or proposed insured, should know the answers. The customer, potential customer, competitor, prospective employee, present employee, or members of the board all have information to offer. The tort victim, the person who claims a contract has been breached, will always work to give clear and completely truthful answers to his or her lawyer.

But independent sources of information are also available to the professional as an essential part of any preinterview investigation. Such sources include credit bureaus (e.g., TRW, Equifax, Dun & Bradstreet), computer databases, court records, property records, the Internet, and the traditional source that is physical evidence.

PHYSICAL EVIDENCE

As we know from crime fiction and movies, physical evidence alone seldom answers all six crucial questions completely. For example, an arson expert can report where a fire occurred and, by examining physical evidence, determine that the fire was, in fact, a case of arson. To answer the more critical question of who set the fire, a professional is required to perform one or more detailed and deep-searching interviews, investigating subjects as to possible motives. Physical evidence, when coupled with a professionally conducted interview, will produce clear answers.

The financial status of a corporation may be found in another source of physical evidence: annual reports or company books. Bookkeepers, however, can create sets of records that, if not entirely falsified, can defy even close analysis. Complete and well-prepared interviews will cut through the "doctored" bookkeeping and uncover the truth. To this end, a forensic accountant or lawyer working with a forensic accountant needs the additional skills of a professional interviewer to obtain enough information to allow the forensic accountant to perform an accurate audit.

In insurance claims cases, it is essential to gather physical evidence and information about the person, buildings, or contents whose risk of loss is insured against. This information is available by personal inspection (viewing) of the property concerned. The information can also be obtained by making personal contacts with the insurance broker or agent; by contacting independent persons; or by viewing the files of the insurer or the corporate records of the company. College transcripts, public records, and personnel files are all important potential sources of preinterview information gathering.

5

Preparing for the Interview

BEFORE THE INTERVIEW BEGINS

Every professional knows that the art of the interview cannot be learned exclusively from the printed word. Conversely, experience alone, without the knowledge and application of general principles, is no assurance of an interviewer's professional development. The adept professional must not only know what these principles are, but also how and when to apply them. Even the simplest technique will occasionally succeed. If the interviewer is to succeed, he or she must know the necessary background information, possess a thoroughly prepared attitude, and, above all, have a plan.

PREPARATION

Gathering Necessary Background Information

Before starting an interview, the professional should know as many facts as possible about the person interviewed and the nature of the investigation. The more the interviewer knows about the subject prior to the interview, the easier it becomes to prepare for the case-specific procedures of an interview.

Data the interviewer should seek out include:

- past insurance claims records;
- criminal records;
- marital status;

- number of children;
- education;
- occupation;
- present job and salary;
- known associates;
- hobbies and interests; or
- any other information pertinent to understanding the subject.

If the interview relates, for example, to an insurance claim, a case of embezzlement, some other form of white-collar crime, or a breach of contract, gathering sufficient background information may be difficult or time consuming, but it is absolutely necessary. Many unskilled interviewers rush in without having done the due diligence of investigative preparation. Within minutes, the subject recognizes that the "professional" has not done his or her homework.

By knowing the facts, the interviewer is in a better position to note discrepancies—and that way, the subject will quickly realize that the interviewer is in possession of all the facts. Simply stated, thorough background knowledge gathered by painstaking preinterview investigation will impress the subject and elicit more information during the course of the interview.

INFORMATION SOURCES: WHERE TO START

As a first step, make contact with other professionals who may have background information on the person to be interviewed. Check with the subject's employer and ask to see his or her personnel file. Privacy protection legislation may prevent you from viewing most of these files unless, of course, the employer is the party against which the claim is being made. Where possible, obtain permission to view such records from the person to be interviewed so that you can look at them beforehand.

If the subject refuses to sign the necessary authorization forms, point out the unequivocal language of the insurance policy or contract, in an effort to compel the subject to provide access to the records. If all else fails, implore the person to be interviewed to help, stressing that a detailed and truthful account is in the best interest of everyone concerned.

Information on the person interviewed may be available from public records, documents in the underwriting files of an existing insurer or prior insurers, personnel files, court files, and records kept by county clerks.

A variety of other sources can be used to unearth this type of information:

- Internet search engines such as Google, Yahoo!, ASK, and Bing are a good place to start looking.
- Commercially available databases such as the INDEX system, PILR (Property Insurance Loss Register), the National Insurance Crime Bureau (NICB) database, County Assessors, and Lexis/Nexis may provide access to Dun & Bradstreet reports, criminal records, and the like.
- Credit reporting agencies like TRW, Equifax, Trans Union, and the Jewelers Board of Trade will yield the subject's credit reports.
- Industry records may contain a wealth of useful information, including the subject's current or past insurance broker, copies of past insurance applications and claims, and information about residency and business locations, property holdings, and health.
- Court records may reveal details of lawsuits, bankruptcy filings, and arrests or convictions.
- Personnel files may contain information on earnings, employment history, work habits, associates, leisure activities, injuries, test results, psychological profiles, and medical conditions.

OTHER SOURCES

The investigation process itself will provide additional sources of potentially useful information that can help the professional get the truth. Although some of these sources are readily available and often quite reliable, unfortunately, professionals seldom use them. Note the benefits and pitfalls inherent in seeking out the following sources.

Neighbors

Any student of human nature will know that people want to talk about their neighbors. A visit by a lawyer or fraud investigator about a neighbor can be exciting for the average person. Influenced by years of television mysteries, the neighbor may be delighted but not surprised by such a visit. People often like to see themselves as part of a drama and—if approached with discretion—will be eager to work studiously to help the investigator.

Proceed with caution, though. In a fraud investigation, for example, unless information gleaned from a neighbor's informal testimony can establish probable guilt, asking the neighbor to sign a recorded statement can be counterproductive. Rather, the professional should conduct an interview and obtain as much information from that interview in as low-key a manner as possible. After the informal interview is completed, if the interviewer finds that the information gathered is significant enough, the relevant points may be formalized with an audio recording or signed written statement.

Neighbors are most useful and reliable when the investigator is corroborating an alibi, verifying the ownership of insured property, or locating other independent parties that may be good sources of information for the professional attempting to establish the occurrence of fraud, breach of contract, or negligence. However, another pitfall of interviewing neighbors is the fact that animosity between neighbors over actual or perceived slights over the years may lead to wrongful accusation.

The professional investigator never relies on a neighbor's statements that cannot later be corroborated. Therefore, the professional should always take a neighbor's most readily delivered accusations with a grain of salt. Granted, such allegations make up part of the background information, but accusations are useless unless they are backed up and corroborated by further investigation.

Insurance Agents or Brokers

The insurance agent or broker is an often-overlooked source of essential information. Agents typically meet with their clients at least once a year, so they know them on a personal level and are familiar with details about their clients' businesses or residences. The broker or agent may be the last person with whom the insured had contact relevant to the case prior to a loss and so can provide and verify the kind of information the professional needs to prove fraud in the inception of a policy.

When meeting with an agent or a broker with regard to a fraud investigation, the professional should obtain the following documents:

- the application for insurance.
- all correspondence between the agent or broker and the insured.
- billing records.
- notes taken by the broker or agent about the insured or the risk.
- photographs taken by the broker.

The professional conducting an insurance fraud investigation should always secure a recorded statement from the agent or broker and, in doing so, should establish whether the relationship to the client is that of an "agent" or that of a "broker." This distinction is important because representations made to or by a broker are considered the responsibility of the insured, whereas representations made to or by an agent are the responsibility of the insurer.

In the recorded statement, the agent or broker should also confirm that all of the questions on the application were asked of the insured and that all of the answers on the application were, in fact, those of the insured.

The Insurer's Inspection Service

Most insurers have a staff of risk assessment engineers. Other insurers hire independent firms to inspect properties insured for the risk of loss and to make reports. These reports are most commonly prepared for commercial risks, but they are also often commonly prepared in high-value residential risk situations.

The reports contain information useful to the professional, such as the following:

- the physical condition of the property at the time of the inspection.
- information that was provided to the inspector by the insured.
- statements by the insured of values at risk.
- hazards observed by the inspector.
- the dimensions of the structure(s).
- materials used in the construction.
- the contents of the structure(s).
- the bookkeeping methods used by the insured.
- the availability of inventory records, sales records, purchase records, and other important documents necessary to establish the amount of loss.

Accountants and Bookkeepers

Because of our increasingly complex tax laws, many people use the services of an accountant or a bookkeeper to keep records of their personal finances or their business. These experts maintain backup records, worksheets, and other data that could be invaluable to the investigative professional in establishing loss or proving fraud.

The professional, after obtaining the proper authorization and consent from the insured or other witness, will seek out this essential information from the witness's accountant or bookkeeper as soon as is practicable after a loss. By obtaining copies of the financial records in a timely manner, the investigating professional will be in a better position to help the insured present a claim or to deter the insured from pursuing further attempts to conceal fraud.

The records to be gathered from an accountant or bookkeeper include:

- tax returns.
- accounting work papers.
- purchase orders, sales invoices, receipts, and physical count inventories.
- profit-and-loss statements.
- balance sheets.
- budgets.
- income and expense projections.

Shopkeepers and Tradespeople

The professional recognizes that some people tend to confide in tradespeople unguardedly and freely—perhaps more freely than they are actually willing to confide in their own friends and relatives or their attorneys. Sitting in a barber's chair, a man might reveal his innermost secrets without the least hesitancy or show of concern. Manicurists often say they learn more from their customers than they would prefer to know. Bartenders often play the role of psychologist to their regular customers. Local business owners hear all kinds of "information" from their customers. When I was an Army Intelligence investigator, I would always visit the local barber, butcher, bartender, and auto mechanic to get a full description of the person being investigated rather than contact the person's friends and relatives.

Unlike formal conversations with a priest or attorney, which are bound by convention and protected by privilege, conversations with hairdressers, bartenders, auto mechanics, or manicurists can be open-ended and information-rich. Often, professionals can obtain more important and detailed background information by interviewing these tradespeople than by spending hours on other forms of research. Clues gained from people who might normally not be considered relevant sources of information can therefore provide the professional with a tactical edge in the interview.

HAVE A PLAN

After learning the background facts concerning the person to be interviewed, as well as the case itself, professionals must formulate a plan. Prior to the interview, they must ask themselves the following questions:

- Why is the interview necessary?
- Why has the person been chosen for interview?
- What does the professional want to learn from the interview?
- What information obtainable through an interview does the interviewer believe the subject has?
- Taking personality into consideration, what is the best method to obtain maximum information from the subject?
- From whom or from what source can additional information be obtained?
- Where will the interview take place?
- When will the interview take place—early morning, afternoon, evening?
- How will the interview be conducted—formally, with a court stenographer, openly or surreptitiously tape-recorded, or informally without a written or audio record?
- In terms of comfort level, and given the character of the person to be interviewed, what should the physical conditions and atmosphere of the interview space be?
- What "type" is the subject—nervous, overwrought, a "cool customer"?
- What tactics would work best with the subject's type?

A plan is different from a mere list of questions prepared before an interview begins. It is an outline reminding the interviewer of all that needs to be uncovered to accomplish the ultimate goal of the interview.

Often even the best-planned tactics prove to be failures under the circumstances of a particular interview, so the professional should be armed with at least four alternative strategies long before the interview begins.

Some interviewers write down all the questions they want to ask, finding this a useful way to organize their thoughts. This method is as acceptable as any, providing that the interviewer, in the frequently difficult course of the interview, is not entirely dependent on (or "married to") the list of prepared questions. Other skilled interviewers, after planning their intended procedure beforehand, take no written notes into the interview. These professionals believe that their apparent reliance on notes or a list of questions both undermines the impression they wish to make on the person to be interviewed and their ability to be effective listeners and flexible interviewers.

LISTEN

The skilled professional listens attentively to the answers obtained from the subject and follows any lead or direction suggested by each answer. The answer to even the first question asked in an interview can lead the professional to other questions and directions not conceived of in the original plan.

If an interviewer merely reads from a list of prepared questions, openings that could lead to potentially vital information will be ignored. The interviewer who does not listen to the subject's answers and adjust the line of questioning accordingly is no more effective than an automaton. A computer could ask the questions just as well. If answers to a prepared list of questions were all that was needed to conduct a successful interview, a questionnaire could be mailed to the subject to fill in at leisure and return. Of course, written questions and answers deprive the interviewer of the ability to see, hear, feel, and smell the body language of the witness. The professional prepares, and prepares well. Starting an interview unprepared is like going fishing without a rod, reel, line, or hook.

No skilled interviewer can afford to be a slave to any preconceived strategy, preparation, or plan. The professional needs to be creative, adapt to the changing thrust and direction of the interview, and, above all, remain resilient in the face of a failed plan.

6

Conducting the Interview

THE IMPORTANCE OF A GOOD OPENING

Public speakers know that an audience is most attentive at the beginning of a speech. The audience always listens with interest and anticipation to the speaker's introductory words. After all, they came to the event because they wanted to learn something from the speaker.

If, however, the speaker's opening salvos augur that the lecture will be boring, the audience soon becomes less and less attentive. Disappointed in the speaker, the audience members begin to regret their decision to attend the event. Once they have fallen into daydreaming, the speaker will find it most difficult to regain their attention, no matter how interesting or how polished the last hour of the talk becomes.

In contrast, if the opening statements suggest the speaker will be interesting and entertaining, the audience will continue to listen throughout the lecture. Skilled public speakers are well aware of this fact, which is why they may devote as much as 4 hours preparing what to say in the first 30 seconds of their talk and only 20 minutes deciding on the content of the remainder of their speech.

Even if the subject feigns unconcern, the professional knows that, at the start of any interview, the subject will be an attentive "audience." The professional also knows that the first words of an interview, like a public speech or performance, strongly influence the success of the rest of the interview. Many novice interviewers make the serious mistake of asking easy, innocuous questions, whose answers are already known to both parties. Unless the subject is extremely nervous or frightened and needs calming before serious questioning can begin, the interview should never begin with questions such as "What is your name?" or "Where do you live?" Such questions immediately signal to the subject that the interviewer is dull or unprepared.

Faced with such queries, the person interviewed thinks, "They don't know anything about me . . . I'm safe!" or "This is a joke!" or "I can tell this person anything I want and he'll believe me," or "They're just stalling for time," or "I have nothing to worry about."

Compare that decidedly less than dynamic beginning with a more direct approach designed to grab and retain the attention and respect of the interviewee:

> Mike, I am Ms. Stevens. There is no question that an arson fire destroyed your house. We know you bought two five-gallon cans full of gasoline the day before the fire. We know there was very little debris remaining in the house after the fire was put out. What did you do with the furniture and artwork you insured?

Similarly, when the interviewer, despite having the due diligence of preinterview investigation, has not been able to gather enough information about what actually happened, he or she can begin the interview with the most important questions. Before the subject has time to consider whether the interviewer actually has the pertinent details, he or she will feel compelled to volunteer information. For example: "Millicent, there was an arson fire at your house. Tell me everything you did the day of the fire."

Or, in a business situation: "Gentlemen, we are here to decide whether our company buys Widget Industries. Tell me everything your research has developed about Widget. The future success of our company rests on the accuracy of your information."

Or, when it is believed the person interviewed was involved in criminal activity: "Are you armed now? Were you armed on the day of the robbery?"

This type of opening, direct and to the point, will more likely result in truthful statements and useful information. It shakes the subject's confidence and immediately puts the subject on the defensive. On the other hand, such an opening will yield mediocre results when used only following a long series of mundane and tangentially relevant questions about the subject's name, occupation, and other everyday details. Therefore, the skilled interviewer will often decide to wait until the end of the interview to ask for statistical details like addresses and ID numbers. The professional interviewer may then choose to confirm this information, but only after having obtained the hard information vital to the investigation and the completion of a successful interview.

Determine your opening statement or line of questioning by first taking into account the background information you have unearthed about the subject and then by making a quick assessment of the subject's attitude upon entering the interview space.

The professional never opens with accusations of guilt, even when the accumulated preinterview evidence appears damning and overwhelming. Such an accusatory tactic can be entirely counterproductive. Rather than ask the subject to admit to the crime or tort itself, the prudent interviewer will ask the subject to admit, one by one, to the elements that combine to establish that a crime, a fraud or a tort, has been committed. For example, when trying to conclude an interview, ask:

- "Isn't it true that you knew the statement you made to your insurance agent was false?"
- "Isn't it true that when you applied for the loan you already knew you had been fired the day before?"
- "Isn't it true that you intended to lie because you knew you couldn't get the insurance if you told the truth?"
- "Isn't it true that you wanted the bank to rely on statements of earnings from your old job in making its decision to loan you money?"
- "Isn't it true that you expected the insurance company to rely on the truth of your statements?"
- "Isn't it true that if the insurance company knew the truth it probably would not have insured you?"
- "Isn't it true you don't have a job?"
- "Isn't it true you can't make the monthly loan payments?"

Finally, note that a professional will approach an independent witness (a person who is not implicated in any wrongdoing but who is thought to have information that could assist the investigation) from a different direction by appealing to a sense of fairness or a spirit of community. Questions directed to an independent witness must necessarily be delivered in a congenial manner that encourages and rewards such cooperative acts of civic or national duty.

KEEP IT ONE-ON-ONE

In most situations, only one interviewer should be in the same room with any individual subject. As we know from hard experience, the true professional has learned that the more people whom the subject knows are listening to his or her testimony, the less chance there is that the subject will be forthcoming with information. Nor should a spouse, relative, friend, or acquaintance of the subject be allowed to participate in, or even sit in on, the interview.

INTRODUCING THE INTERVIEWER

When the interviewer meets the person to be interviewed for the first time, it is best to introduce himself or herself as "Mr. Williams" or "Ms. Forth" (or even as "Bill Williams" or "Sally Forth") instead of "Investigator This" or "Special Agent That" or "Attorney Mason."

Any professional title that the interviewer may (understandably) be proud of in daily life could prove an intimidating factor in the interview situation. Titles tend to point too directly to the investigative purpose of the interview, while given names pose no such social barrier. In this way, the investigator puts the subject at ease, and the interview can proceed more like a natural conversation than an interrogation.

Use Titles Sparingly

The use of titles almost always accomplishes nothing. Similarly, it is best not to mention the official units or departments that the interviewer may belong to or represent. Mentioning the "fraud unit" or the "internal audit department" or law firm serves only to intimidate the interview subject.

Since persuasion and salesmanship are key to a successful interview, it is best to remove such references and defuse the formal atmosphere as much as possible. The subject should be made to feel that the interviewer, far from wanting to exercise his or her putative authority, is interested only in gathering the necessary facts to help prove a claim, acquire a policy, or retain a job. An interviewer who introduces herself as "Lawyer Williams" is perceived far differently than the one who wishes to be addressed simply as Sally Williams. Though they are one and the same person, the "Lawyer" will be seen as a person to be feared, whereas "Sally" will be felt to be an equal.

The interviewer's business card should also not display titles. The ubiquitous business card impresses no one nowadays. If used at all, it should provide only the basic information of name, address, telephone number, and e-mail address. In this way, the subject will be left to make his or her own assumptions about any position of importance the interviewer might hold.

As with all aspects of the interviewing art, though, flexibility is king, and this advice may be inverted when it suits the case at hand. Through the *de rigueur* process and due diligence of background investigation, it may be known that a particular subject responds positively to the signifiers of position or rank—to titles and authority figures in general—and an interviewer might find it more effective to play on such tendencies in the subject when making his or her self-introduction. For instance, a pompous, egotistical subject might be much more cooperative when being questioned by some impressively titled person of importance in the company. Such a self-centered individual would consider it unseemly to be talking with anyone who was not a "big shot." Therefore, he or she might refuse to give any information to a lowly lawyer, broker, or safety engineer. This person will, however, readily confide in a claims manager, a vice president of internal audit, or a law firm's managing partner. Similarly, a military general would likely hold second lieutenants in contempt and would never confide in any junior officer, but conditioned by military hierarchy, he or she would feel compelled to speak truthfully to a special agent of the U.S. Army Intelligence Corps or a high-ranking officer of the U.S. Army Criminal Investigation Division.

Address the Person Interviewed Strategically

The professional most often addresses the interview subject by the interviewee's first name unless the professional perceives that addressing the person interviewed by a title and a surname will be advantageous.

For example, when Mrs. Louise Uppercrust, a snooty and pretentious socialite, appears to give testimony, the interviewer does not address her in the manner of a headwaiter showing a valued customer to a reserved ringside table in a swank nightclub. To address her as "Mrs. Uppercrust" or even as "Madame" tells the socialite that her power and authority are what control the situation, here as elsewhere. Addressed in the respectful language that she's accustomed to, she will assume control of the interview and place the interviewer on a lower social rung. Instead, the experienced professional starts the interview by saying, "Louise, I am Mr. Simmons."

Mrs. Uppercrust is not used to anyone she does not consider her social equal calling her "Louise." She certainly would never condescend to use a title like "Mr." with someone who is so obviously her social inferior. The interviewer has politely but firmly set the tone by establishing a new social order in the interview: one to which Louise Uppercrust must now defer.

The informality tactic does not mean that the interviewer should ever call her "Lu," "Lulu," or "Louzie," for that would be overdoing it, but a leveling of the social playing field will go a long way to establishing equality and conveying the interviewer's expectations.

The same principle applies to Dr. John Orthosurgeon. To address him as "Doctor" could give him a sense of relative status that is of no advantage to the interviewer. Rather, the professional calls him "John" in a polite but familiar tone that assumes and implies that both parties are on an equal social footing.

The reverse principle is true when dealing with subjects whose occupations may give them the sense that they are of low social standing. For example, janitors, cleaners, or convenience store clerks are commonly subjected to rudeness and indignities by thoughtless customers or employers. To be suddenly addressed as "Mr. Brown" or "Mrs. Robb" will cause them to think more highly of both themselves and the interviewer. Having thus had their self-esteem gently elevated, subjects will be much more likely to be forthcoming and cooperative than if the interviewer were to talk down to them.

Appear Amiable but Firm

As we have pointed out, no professional can ever succeed without developing a friendly demeanor. The ability to speak in tones conducive to natural and open conversation helps create an atmosphere of friendliness, an ability that the skilled interviewer can turn to an advantage in the interview's often lengthy search for truth.

Nevertheless, the true professional does not fail to be firm with the subject whenever necessary. The interviewer must do so, however, in a way that the subject respects. The person interviewed should not begin to feel animosity toward the interviewer but, rather, should come to respect such firm resolve as a sign of true professionalism and a quality worthy of respect.

By showing and, in turn, expecting respect, the interviewer can avoid generating any negative atmosphere that can emerge when the interviewer harbors dislike of (or even genuine contempt for) the subject. Creating this ideal atmosphere of mutual respect of course requires that the interviewer possess an even temper. Most subjects will quickly lose respect for the professional who is unable to control his or her temper.

Never Lose Your Temper

When the interviewer's temper flares, he or she can no longer think ahead clearly nor logically follow the interview plan. An outburst of temper makes redesigning the interview strategy next to impossible. As a result, far from gaining more control over the subject and the interview process, the interviewer "loses control" in both senses of the term.

A show of temper degrades the interviewer in the eyes of the subject. Similarly, while the ploy of self-deprecation may work in gaining the ear of a colleague or friend, it seldom works to further the success of an interview if used on a subject. When I was a young investigator, I learned this lesson forcefully when I made the mistake of referring to a subject as a "son of a bitch," only to cause him to explode with violence and curses, quickly turning a potential witness into a enemy.

The interviewer must remember that the subject is always, in some sense, an adversary in the interview session, even though the professional is playing the role of advocate for the subject. Too much self-deprecating humor on the part of the interviewer can cause the subject to lose some degree of respect for the interviewer.

If, however, the interviewee is so full of hubris that any indication of a lack of skill or intelligence in the interviewer will please the interviewee, it may be effective to convey ineptitude. As a result, the subject often becomes less cautious and proceeds to make admissions that would not be made to an interviewer perceived as a professional. Arrogant, self-aggrandizing subjects, perceiving modesty as weakness in the interviewer may even try to "educate" the interviewer, thus revealing the sought-after information more readily. But this strategy rarely works.

Obviously, and for similar reasons, the interviewer who conveys an air of self-importance may find that the strategy backfires in many cases. Bragging and inflated bravado, especially with regard to training, skill, or position of authority, most often results in a loss of respect and cooperation even more quickly than the tactic of mild self-deprecating humor.

Be Alert, Observe, Determine Action

What may feel like intuition in the interview process is actually the guiding effect of cumulative experience. This subconscious sense of guidance is often called a "hunch," but there is nothing mysterious or clairvoyant about it. It is simply applied experience at work. The professional interviewer knows that years of experience and the application of painstakingly acquired powers of observation subconsciously guide him or her in any interview.

Any initial contact between two people involves a kind of mutual evaluation. Even without all the facts, one tends to make assumptions about the other person, based on similar past meetings and similar experiences. Being derived from first impressions, these assumptions should not constitute an actual conclusion, but they do become a working template for ongoing interactions. This learned ability to make instant evaluations is a subconscious effect of cumulative experience. The interview professional, being far more adept than most people, can evaluate a subject based on the experience of hundreds of interviews.

- "He just doesn't seem honest."
- "I wouldn't trust her with a 50-cent piece."
- "I think he's a big phony."
- "I liked him the first time I met him."
- "She's a nice person."

Gesture, word, vocal inflection, and posture—the skilled interviewer is attuned to all these indications and more. A sullen manner or a defensive attitude tells the true professional just as much as a lighthearted smile or a straightforward response. Drawing from any and all of these indications, the skilled professional makes a temporary "working-copy" evaluation. The interviewer is careful not to draw any final conclusion from this initial evaluation, but instead tests it out as he or she proceeds. Even after years of interview experience, the interviewer does not assume that he or she knows the interviewee like a parent would know a child. The true professional has long ago learned there is much more to it than that.

A subject may appear angry or at ease, upset or unconcerned, reticent or talkative. Rather than take such outward behavior at face value, the interviewer must first determine whether the interviewee is feigning an emotion or revealing honest feelings. A subject may be trying to bluff by adopting the righteous anger of an innocent person falsely accused. It takes an alert, constantly observant interviewer to determine the difference.

Gender conditioning can also affect the ability of the less skilled interviewer to discern the authenticity of the subject's mood. For instance, a male interviewer may be dismayed or bemused if a woman cries during an interview, whereas a female interviewer may not be fazed by such behavior or, alternatively, may be able to provide a more sympathetic response than would a male interviewer.

From the initial quick character evaluation, skilled interviewers are then able to determine their opening statement, question, or strategy. The clues obtained from initial observation in effect determine how the interviewer is going to begin the interview. Throughout the interview, the professional remains alert to any changes in the subject that require concurrent changes in the techniques being applied. A successful interviewer is consciously and continually alert to all the signs that indicate changes in the emotions and thoughts of the subject.

Some physical clues to look for that might indicate that a subject is being untruthful include:

- dry mouth.
- restlessness—frequent changes of position.
- immobility.
- foot-tapping or finger-drumming.
- excessive perspiration.

- excessive swallowing.
- avoidance of eye contact with the interviewer.
- repeated use of phrases that attempt to demonstrate truthfulness:
    - "To tell you the truth"
    - "As God is my witness, this is true"

None of these indicators guarantees that the subject is being untruthful. They are significant, however, in that they reveal that the interview process is having an effect on the subject. The professional interviewer, noting these signs, knows to play on the subject's stress. The professional may then continue with renewed vigor and attention, posing direct questions at an accelerated pace in order to deprive the subject of any opportunity to fabricate lies. Or the interviewer may ask no questions or may allow long silences—while holding the gaze of the person interviewed—in order to allow the subject's fears to grow.

MISDIRECTION AND INDIRECT QUESTIONING

Every professional interviewer is adept at using the technique of indirect questioning to obtain information. Indirect questioning is often the best technique, and sometimes the only one, that will work. The professional poses what appear to be innocuous questions in a way that conceals the real purpose behind them. Such questions are acutely purposeful: they are designed to appear unimportant, as if the interviewer is just making friendly conversation. From the point of view of the subject, they should appear to have little or no bearing on the case.

The skilled interviewer operates with the knowledge that seemingly inept, offhand, casually delivered questions frequently help produce information that leads to the truth. The professional gains proficiency in this technique by constantly developing a taste and a talent for small talk. You can conduct informal information-gathering interviews with subjects anywhere, whether they be chats in hallways or conversations at the coffee machine—wherever the subject does not expect or believe the interaction to be of the "official" interview type.

Indirect questioning involves two commingled factors: word phrasing and delivery.

DELIVERY

The importance of your choice of words, and the effect of your delivery, can be illustrated by the variety of uses to which a common word like "you" can be put. That word, when shouted in your direction in a strange town by a police officer, would make you feel apprehensive and compel you to stop in your tracks. "You" uttered sweetly by one lover to another would convey a completely different meaning. The word is the same; the important difference between them is the delivery.

The interviewer's expression of indifference will prick the ego of the person interviewed who is suspected of being an embezzler or fraud perpetrator and cause the interviewee to explain how effective he or she was at committing the fraud. Details on how the embezzlement was perpetrated will flow from the person interviewed before the person realizes that wrongdoing was admitted.

WORD CHOICE AND PHRASING

The skilled interviewer should try to employ the relevant terminology that insurance professionals (or art appraisers or construction engineers, as the case may be) would use. Understanding what the interviewer is referring to, the interviewee will recognize that he or she has some knowledge of the field.

Interviewers who have a studied facility with word choice and a subtle sense of phrasing can convey to the subject their doubts regarding the subject's claim of expertise, without insulting him or her. Faced with such articulate delivery, subjects will be anxious to match the interviewer with their own demonstration of specialized expertise in order to prove competence. Even persons making a fraudulent claim of art theft will be eager to show off their years of art expertise.

THE BACKHANDED COMPLIMENT

In comedies, we laugh when we see actors barricading a door by piling on chairs, tables, and sofas to keep out an assailant who then comes through an open window. This is very similar to the techniques of misdirection that a skilled interviewer uses to divert attention or throw a subject off guard.

As an interviewer walks into a room to conduct an investigation into a burglary case, he senses immediate antagonism from the person to be interviewed. The interviewer begins the interview with:

> "I don't know why they consider *you* a suspect. This is way out of your line. This job took guts and brains. Taken were diamonds, a mink jacket, and expensive stuff an amateur like you wouldn't know how to pawn or fence. Look at you! In those clothes you look so damn seedy you should be arrested for vagrancy!"
>
> "Like hell, that night I had on my good suit."

The subject's response, to his immediate regret and ultimate detriment, turned into an admission.

The prideful subject, clearly more concerned with a perceived insult contained in the interviewer's cleverly delivered misdirection than with keeping mum, lets down his guard. Tricked by a simple ruse, despite all intentions to the contrary, he admits participation in the crime. One second too late he realizes he fell into the trap that the carefully delivered misdirection can set.

MAKE ONLY PROMISES YOU CAN KEEP

The professional never makes a promise that cannot be fulfilled. An interviewer will lose all credibility if the subject perceives that the interviewer does not have the power to effect terms or conditions that he or she vows are guaranteed.

Just as a physician will never promise a patient a cure, the professional dealing with an insurance claim, a tort, or a breach of contract will never promise the claimant that giving a confession will result in payment. When interviewing for an embezzlement case or other potential crime, no professional will ever promise criminal immunity.

If asked, the interviewer must say:

> I have no power to make any promises in regard to payment of a claim, immunity from prosecution, or a lesser sentence if you decide to tell the truth.
>
> I could tell you that you won't be arrested or go to jail, but that would be lying to you. I haven't told you any lies here today, and I'm not going to start now. Those things are out of my hands. I'm only here to find out exactly what happened.

The subject may be looking for assurance and promises, but if the interviewer is caught out in a meaningless promise, all the interviewer's hard work will be for naught.

When an interviewer honestly tells the subject at the outset that promises of leniency from other authorities cannot be made, the subject enters the interview knowing that the interviewer is not going to attempt tricks or practice deception. This may help to overcome a criminal subject's natural distrust of investigators. With his or her trust in the interviewer reinforced, the subject becomes increasingly likely to tell the truth with every urging by the interviewer.

The tone conveyed is as important as the words spoken. The person interviewed must be convinced that the interviewer is interested only in saving him or her from even more serious problems.

An insurance agent or a broker should never promise to get the person interviewed a policy that "covers everything." Rather, the professional, in the role of broker or agent, should tell the potential insured, "I will try to get you the best policy I can. No policy covers everything. Some cover more than others. With total information—absolute truth—I can get you the best coverage available."

This type of prudence is not employed solely for purposes of interview strategy: if false promises are made, the insured could later bind the insurer to coverage not intended and a lawsuit, in the event a loss resulted from a peril not covered by the policy. The hard-won truth will become legally and practically *tainted,* and the hours of interview time will be rendered less than useless.

The interviewer who makes a false promise is simply dishonest and will be perceived as such. This is especially true in cases where a person confesses to some criminal activity after being promised leniency or a "not guilty" decision. In the courts, prosecutors are not allowed to use confessions gained in this manner. A prudent judge, learning how the confession was obtained, will dismiss the case. The United States is a litigious society, and it is common knowledge that false promises made to gain information will destroy a legitimate defense in a jury trial, too, once it becomes apparent that the investigating party acted unprofessionally.

7

Control

Usually, a professional interviewer is not called to a location (whether the scene of a crime or the location of an insurance claim or other event) until days or weeks after the precipitating event. The person who has committed insurance fraud, embezzlement, other business fraud, breached a contract, or injured someone tortiously, almost certainly has had a great deal of time to plan the crime. Furthermore, the criminal/subject has had ample time to prepare and practice the responses designed to convince the investigator of his or her innocence.

In a first step to gain some modicum of control over any investigative situation, the professional interviewer must be as prepared as possible for the intricate stories that the subject will try to employ in an effort to clear him- or herself of suspicion.

Even though the criminal has had time to weave a fabric of credible lies, he or she is always acutely aware that the fictionalized account is imperfect. The criminal, knowing the actual truth, is extremely conscious of the story's faults and fears the interviewer will also be able to see them; the skilled interviewer will not disabuse the subject of that misunderstanding.

In a sense, any criminal expects to be caught, and that is already the first measure of control that the professional enjoys. First-time perpetrators of fraud often expect that, at worst, they will be able to walk away from the fraud investigation with just the loss of their claim and suffer no penalty. Criminals can be emboldened by the general assumption that most businesses do not wish to experience the embarrassment and bad press that accompany their admission to having been the victims of fraud. However, the skilled interviewer can easily shatter such incorrect assumptions.

In cases where the comfortable and quiet interview does not result in information, control of the person being interviewed should be both emotional and physical. Even before establishing basic rapport with the person interviewed, the professional makes it clear that the two are not having a friendly conversation and that he or she expects answers to all the questions posed.

RAPID-FIRE QUESTIONING TO EFFECT CONTROL

The importance of the professional's maintenance of control in the interview process cannot be overemphasized. A clear plan of action and an insistence—within reason—that the subject be willing to be led through the plan of action are essential. Simply stated, this means that the interviewer asks the questions and the subject answers them.

In addition to physical methods of control (e.g., the furniture and layout of a room, closeness of the interviewer to the subject), the interviewer can first establish a degree of control by asking a series of short, direct, yes–no questions. By following one question with another, without pause, the person interviewed has time only to answer the question posed rather than to elaborate with further fabrications, interject questions, or sidetrack the interview. Constraining response time in this way is an effective interview tool: it prevents the person interviewed from creating plausible false answers. Only thorough preparation, however, enables the interviewer to have these rapid-fire questions ready to go at a moment's notice.

Depending on the interviewer's evaluation of the subject, some narrative responses that ramble and say nothing should be discouraged until control is established. The interview that has developed a great deal of information through narrative responses will often conclude with questions that call for a yes–no response, *if* it would be useful to the search for the truth.

The skillful interviewer learns from practical experience when it is time to begin seeking and encouraging narrative responses in the interview. After some level of control has been established, the interviewer will let the subject feel at liberty to answer questions at length. The astute interviewer listens closely and allows the narrative(s) to continue, but always reestablishes control with short, specific questions whenever salient points in the narrative call for closer examination.

Each short and specific question should address only a single point and not be conjoined with other points the interviewer wishes to confirm. In dealing with particularly recalcitrant types—those who are habitually and stubbornly defiant of authority or attempts at guidance—the short, quick yes–no questions are often the most, if not the *only*, effective tool.

It takes practice for the interviewer to overcome personal communication habits and to speak only in short, yes–no, or direct substantive questions. The technique compels the person interviewed to reply with simple declarative answers. At the appropriate time, the interviewer should ask questions such as the following in a rapid fashion so that the person interviewed has little or no time to craft false answers.

- "Were you home last night?"
- "What time did you arrive?"
- "How long were you there?"
- "When did you leave home?"
- "When did you arrive at work?"
- "Did you set the alarm?"
- "Did you disarm the alarm system?"
- "Did you arm the alarm system before you left work?"
- "Did you drive home?"
- "How long did it take you?"
- "Did you return to work?"
- "How long did it take?"
- "Where were you at 2:12 a.m.?"
- "How did you learn about the fire?"
- "Where were you when you were told?"
- "Were you fired from your last job?"
- "Were you paid more than $100,000 a year at your last job?"

THE FORMAL INTERVIEW

There should never be a telephone in the room where the interview takes place, and the subject should be required to shut off his or her cell phone. The room should include only two people: the subject and the interviewer. Even expected amenities for the comfort of the person interviewed, such as water, coffee, or soft drinks, should not be provided there.

The interview room itself, like those used by police investigators, should be small and windowless, with space sufficient only for two people to sit at a small table. The walls should be bare: there should be no photos, prints, posters, or artwork to distract or relax the person to be interviewed. Neither should the room be stocked with newspapers, magazines, or any other reading material. There should just be four bare, neutral-colored walls. The lighting should be nondiffused fluorescent. The chairs should be as basic as possible.

Seating arrangements are also key. The interviewer should sit at the corner of the table, close enough to be able to touch the person interviewed. By doing so, he or she encroaches on the subject's comfort zone, a dynamic that increases the degree of control. In this deliberately adjacent seating arrangement, the entire body of the subject will be visible to the interviewer, and those critical clues of body language we mentioned before can be observed. The subject's chair could have slightly uneven legs (easily accomplished by removing the rubber cap from one leg) which will add further to the atmosphere of discomfort. The interviewer's chair may be slightly but perceptibly higher than the chair the subject is asked to sit in to give the interviewer an appearance of height, looking down on the witness.

The psychological impact of initially (and/or occasionally) leaving a subject alone in the interview room can be a strong one and useful in establishing control. Ten minutes waiting alone, prior to an interview, can significantly increase the subject's discomfort level without giving the appearance that any malice was intended. When the fresh, confident, businesslike interviewer finally walks in, the subject will already be tired and will be much more willing to provide answers in order to "just get through" the interview.

If the interviewer walks in and finds the subject sitting in the wrong chair, or if the subject does not rise when the interviewer enters the room, the interviewer can say, "George, I have a bad back, and that's my special chair you are sitting in. Do you mind sitting in the other one?"

Such a request may seem trivial, but by unhesitatingly asking to switch chairs—especially if the chairs appear to be identical—the interviewer instantly establishes a certain measure of control.

THE HOME/WORKPLACE INTERVIEW

If the interview must take place in the home or place of business of the person to be interviewed, the skilled professional can still take some control over what will occur in this less formal environment. It is important, however, that the interviewer not *appear* to be taking control; rather, the interviewer must be respectful of the subject's home or workplace and maintain propriety. The interviewer will request, seemingly for the benefit of the subject, that the interview take place in a single room with adequate privacy and will further ask that the telephones be disconnected or set to "do not disturb" mode. Often, a skilled interviewer will suggest the "best" place to sit before the host/subject has a chance to do so. The interviewer might propose that the interview be conducted at a desk or table, if it is believed that a sense of opposition or separation will play on the nerves of the subject. Or a low sofa might be selected for the host. The interviewer then might switch to a standard chair, allowing the interviewer to "look down upon" the subject. As in the formal interview, the closeness and relative position of the two participants is a factor over which the interviewer can exert some control, even when entering the subject's home or work environment.

With these techniques in mind, the interviewer can at every step work to assume control. All of the following factors can combine to provide the interviewer with a marked advantage over the subject in any interview:

- The subject has something to lose or gain from the interview.
- The subject does not know how much the interviewer knows.
- The subject can be made to wait for the interviewer.
- The subject is to be interviewed in a special room.
- The subject cannot be sure of the outcome of the interview.
- The subject can be unnerved by a confident, skilled interviewer.
- The subject knows that his or her decisions can be personally beneficial or harmful.

THE NO-COMFORT ZONE: THE POLICE INTERVIEW

A cardinal rule when conducting a police interview is that no comfort be offered to the person interviewed. Professionals who are not law enforcement officers are somewhat more limited in the range of techniques described here. But the techniques of the police interview may be modified, toned down, and adapted to fit the civil interview.

When adhering to the no-comfort rule, a police interviewer will not allow a subject to drink beverages or to smoke during an interview. Given the rise in the number of nonsmokers in recent years, tobacco deprivation may have become passé as an interviewing weapon. Still, it is instructive to examine how police interviewers make use of this technique.

Those who smoke, or have smoked, know the psychological value of offering a cigarette to a person truly addicted to tobacco, and the powerful effect of depriving the person of it. Many years ago, when cigarette companies were allowed to advertise on television, a cigarette advertisement instructed the smoker: "When embarrassed, be nonchalant and light up." Police interviewers know that allowing a subject to light up a cigarette affords an opportunity to relax and create plausible lies. Depriving the person interviewed of a cigarette provides no such "break," and the subject's stress level and fatigue increase as the symptoms of withdrawal set in.

Ritualistically removing a cigarette from the pack, tamping down the tobacco, lighting it, and exhaling the first puff provide the person being interviewed 20 to 30 seconds to create a credible—though entirely dishonest—response to a difficult question. This is why police conduct interviews "down at the station" where strict no-smoking (and other) regulations exist, rather than in the uncontrolled environment of the subject's home.

Prevented from smoking for an hour or more, the nicotine addict begins to experience mild withdrawal symptoms. Some police investigators steadfastly maintain that this need for nicotine alone can compel smokers to give confessions, if only to avoid the discomfort of being without the drug. There is no hard evidence to support such a claim, however, any more than there is proof that depriving a person of coffee or alcohol is effective. Police interrogators simply know that, according to the no-comfort philosophy, the very act of allowing a subject moments in which to relax and reflect diminishes the interviewer's power and shifts the impetus of control over to the subject. Moreover, the train of questioning can be lost, and the subject might even reclaim some personal space and control by blowing smoke in the direction of the interviewer.

A police interviewer will say whatever is convenient to enforce the "no comfort, no smoking" tenet. If necessary, the police interviewer will claim to be asthmatic or to have a violent allergy to cigarette smoke. If he or she determines that a subject is a smoker (either by the smell of the subject's breath, telltale yellowed fingertips, a pack of cigarettes in the breast pocket, or a direct request for a cigarette), such knowledge gives the interviewer a potential advantage. When the person interviewed starts to reach for a cigarette, the police interviewer will say something like, "Okay, Joe, tell me the truth here and you can go out and have a smoke. We can't smoke in here because of fire regulations."

Or the officer might say, "Dianne, tell me what I want to know and you can go out and have a smoke. This is a smoke-free facility and we can't let anyone smoke in here." The interviewer does not just bluntly tell the subject that there is no smoking allowed in the interview space, but instead offers the possibility as a concession for cooperation.

In these days of widespread antismoking sentiment, refusing to let a person smoke in an "official" place will increasingly be seen as normal and reasonable. Naturally, the professional interviewer does not risk causing animosity by smoking in the interview session either.

As with every strategy, however, there is always the other side of the coin. In fact, there are times when the police interviewer will see the advantages of permitting a subject to smoke. The sharp police interviewer will choose to offer a cigarette when:

- The subject has been physically mistreated in some way prior to the interview.
- The subject has been verbally abused by another interviewer or third party.
- The subject, denied the privilege of smoking, has become uncommunicative.
- The subject is obviously distraught and is incapable of being coherent.

The perceptible calming effect of a cigarette—especially one that was previously forbidden—will quickly gain the interviewer a great advantage.

DIFFERENT PROCEDURES: CIVIL INVESTIGATION

Lacking the powers of threat of arrest or detention, the professional conducting a civil investigation must find other ways to be seen as a person with the power to help the subject achieve his or her goal.

Police interviews are often conducted by pairs of officers, and allowing concessions contrary to the rules is one of the innumerable variations on the well-known (infamous, even) "good cop/bad cop" routine. When a second interviewer enters the room, he or she might say, "Ralph, smoking is not allowed in here, but if you want a cigarette, go ahead. Better just have one, though. Regulations, you know. Just don't tell anyone I'm breaking the rules to help you."

Obviously, permitting the subject to smoke can make the subject more kindly disposed toward the interviewer. The noncommissioned interviewer, too, can modify such familiar police techniques of restriction and permission to use on the person interviewed. The professional must, above all, exude an aura of good faith and fair dealing. Part of the process of creating such an atmosphere without giving up control of the interview is to adopt an approach quite different from that used by police investigators. The professional must take care not to deny the subject any comforts and must establish the most conducive atmosphere possible.

The professional should never appear prosecutorial and must never give the appearance of working for, or with, a police agency. Instead of depriving a subject of the right to a cigarette or forcing the subject to sit in an uncomfortable chair, the professional's tactic in civil investigations is to disarm and overwhelm by kind consideration. The professional will offer coffee, tea, decaf, water, nonalcoholic beverages—anything the subject is likely to want. The skilled interviewer is also sensitive to any additional needs that may arise during the course of the interview. These things are not done out of any quality of kindness unique to interviewers but purely to use the most effective proven strategies in civil investigations.

When the interviewer in a civil case makes the person interviewed comfortable, the process is certain to take far longer to complete than no-comfort police interviews, which can sometimes be extremely efficient. This is a fact of life for the professional, who cannot operate behind the power of a badge. Sometimes a civil interview will take less than 30 minutes, and sometimes it will proceed over a period of days or even weeks, with intervals between. The patient, skilled interviewer will work through each case situation, concerned only with a positive outcome and entirely untroubled about time.

Granted, heavy-handed police techniques, if they do not result in the case being thrown out of court, sometimes obtain results more quickly, but similar attempts by the civil interviewer will lead to mistrust and charges of bad faith. Only by creating a comfortable atmosphere and taking all the time in the world can professional interviewers enjoy every confidence that they will achieve the desired results.

USE OF A SECOND INTERVIEWER

There are occasions when an interviewer, despite expertise acquired from years of interview study and experience, cannot get the necessary information from a particular subject. In such cases, a second interviewer can be used as a replacement. Ideally, such a substitute interviewer will have been listening to the interview, out of sight and unbeknownst to the subject, or will at least be familiar with the particulars (and the particular problems) of the interview case. Many times the second interviewer can obtain information because his or her personality just happens to be better suited to the personality of the subject than that of the original interviewer. Of course, a good interviewer always tries to adjust his or her manner in order to project the most effective interview personality, but human variables are seemingly unlimited, and a second interviewer may save time and effort.

The second interviewer, having witnessed the attempts to elicit information from the subject, may employ approaches that the first interviewer, having been so thoroughly engaged in using the chosen interview strategies, may have overlooked. In addition, a second interviewer who has witnessed the interview from outside the room has the advantage of knowing that repetition of failed techniques would have disastrous results.

For example, if the first interviewer unsuccessfully used the "You look like my younger brother" approach, then the adept second interviewer would never use the same approach on the person interviewed.

It would make an impression, however, if the second interviewer were to say:

> Gee, you know, Bill, you look a lot like John's younger brother. [Pause.] I wonder if that's why he seems to be taking such an interest in you. Usually he is very short-tempered. He told me he prefers it when he can catch subjects lying, so he can make sure they are punished. But he's taking more time than usual with you. Yeah . . . must be because you remind him of his younger brother."

The timing for introducing a second interviewer depends on the dynamics and particulars of each interview. In some interviews, an impasse may become obvious after only five minutes; in others, it may take two hours before the principal interviewer decides help is needed. If the first interviewer and the subject take an immediate dislike to each other—or develop it over the course of the interview—it serves no practical purpose to continue with that interview pairing. Despite all the interviewer's diplomacy and self-control, the feeling of animosity will obstruct the process.

The astute interviewer, sensing it is time to bring in a second interviewer, will ask the subject if he or she would like something to eat or drink, or if the subject would like to go to the toilet, for example. This can provide a plausible opportunity to bring in a second interviewer, and the less abrupt transition to a second interviewer will seem more natural.

Should the subject turn down any such offers, the interviewer could simply leave the room, implying that he or she would like to get a beverage or take a bathroom break.

When left alone in the interview room, most people begin to "sweat." Subjects begin to worry about what the interviewer is doing or saying out of their presence.

APPROACHES FOR A SECOND INTERVIEWER

The following are some of the openings available to the second interviewer working on a potential criminal insurance fraud. The techniques presented here are directed toward investigating a crime and should be used only with extreme caution in any other type of interview situation.

The Accusatory Approach

A second interviewer can be called in briefly to take a much stronger, more accusatory, and intimidating tone with the subject. After perfunctory introductions, the second interviewer might say:

> "Are you a relative of (name of first interviewer)?"
>
> "No? Oh, then you must be an old friend of his?"
>
> "No? Well then, tell me, why is he taking so much time with you?"
>
> Or he or she might say:
>
> Bill, I am in here because I am making an extensive study of congenital liars. How many people in your family have been treated by a psychiatrist? None? Well, the way you are acting in here, we're beginning to think you may need treatment. In a serious situation like this, a normal person would realize that the best thing to do is to tell the truth. But here you are, insisting on *not* telling the truth. That just leaves us with one conclusion: you don't know how to tell the truth about anything. Now tell me, when was the first time that a doctor told you that you needed psychiatric treatment?

Or the second interviewer might ask:

> Lou, do you know what the true *criminal type* is? It's the type of person who doesn't tell the truth when the chips are down. I'm afraid that's where you have put yourself. The chips *are* down, and you have put yourself on the side of the enemies of society. When it comes time for sentencing, judges can always spot the criminal type, and they can always see the honest guy who just made a mistake and who deserves a break.

When an interviewer is extremely confident that the subject is lying, he or she might say:

> I hope you continue to lie to me, Susan. Keep up the good work. As long as you keep saying that you don't know anything about this, when we know perfectly well that you do, we can only conclude that you are criminally minded. We thought this was just going to be a simple insurance claim interview. In cases like this, companies can force you to stay in court with them for years.

After using this technique for a few minutes, the second interviewer might then leave the interview room to be replaced by the original interviewer, whom the subject now views somewhat more sympathetically.

The "Good Cop/Bad Cop" Technique

When the original interviewer returns, he or she might say:

> Sorry, that was my boss. He seems determined to find you guilty of fraud here, doesn't he? But you know, I don't care what he says. I just want to help you get the truth out so we can all go home. You've got a family, just like I have, and you don't want to be wasting time here. Let's just go over some of the details again and see if we can't wrap this thing up.

The subject now sees the interviewer in a more favorable light than before. Out of appreciation for the "good" interviewer, and in the realization that he or she is right about the benefits of telling the truth, many subjects decide to tell the interviewer the entire story.

In formal examinations under oath, or deposition testimony including the presence of a court reporter, the experienced interviewer can, in the same way, appear to the subject to be an ally, a "good cop" there for support.

While these and many more variations on the "good cop/bad cop" technique are well known to the public, in practice the technique does not seem to have suffered from its overuse in television dramas. It remains a standard throughout the world.

TIME IS TORTUROUS

At the outset of the interview, the professional should make the subject understand that there is no time limit involved. Granted, the subject is not under house arrest and there may be valid reasons why an interview has a time limit. The person interviewed, however, must be convinced that the interviewer is in no rush to complete the process and will be patient and persistent until the truth is revealed.

Knowing this, the subject begins—even from the start of the interview—to be worn down by the process. When subjects eventually become exhausted from answering questions, they can lose track of the lies told, or they can give up their effort to keep their lies consistent and coherent. Time is to the interviewer's advantage: to escape this discomfort, the subject will take the only avenue of escape and tell the truth.

Real physical torture will get answers, but the answers gained will not necessarily be the truth. In medieval times, devices such as the rack or the thumbscrew were used, but modern professionals now recognize that such abhorrent and illegal practices do not compel the persons accused to give the truth, but only to say whatever they believe will stop the torturing.

Psychological techniques, in combination with canny interview skills, will often obtain reliable results when the interviewer takes the tortuous time necessary to make them work.

8

Dealing with Types

CHANGING THE SUBJECT'S EMOTIONS

No two interviews are the same. Interview techniques that work with one subject may be useless with another. In order to determine the whole truth from an interview, the subject must sometimes be guided into the right frame of mind. At the start of the interview, it is often necessary for the skilled interviewer to positively affect the emotional state of the person interviewed. Although the interviewer is always in control, letting the person being interviewed believe that he or she is in control of the process may sometimes be effective.

Quickly obtaining the truth from an obviously distraught individual could prove impossible. Subjects in states of melancholy or despair may be unresponsive to, or unmoved by, the interviewer's standard appeals. Single-word responses may be all that such subjects are capable of providing. The interviewer needs to work to convince the person interviewed that things are not as serious, difficult, or desperate as he or she thinks they are. In these cases, rather than launching into the hard and pointed questions of the interview, the skilled professional takes great care to first establish a genuine rapport with the person interviewed by taking time to inquire about family, work, and shared interests.

THE HIGHLY EMOTIONAL PERSON

When dealing with any extremely upset person, the skilled interviewer exploits the subject's emotional state. The interviewer points out that the only way to achieve calm is to reveal the truth.

For example, the interviewer might say reassuringly:

> Sue, this isn't one-tenth as bad as you think. I talk to people every day about things a lot more serious things than this. So you tried to cheat your insurance company and you didn't succeed, but this is a very minor case. Lots of people have tried the same thing. Tell me the truth, and I'll see if I can help.

Or the interviewer might say sympathetically:

> I'm talking with you since I'm sure you don't want to feel like you do now the rest of your life. You will continue to feel terrible until you just tell the truth. Why will you continue to feel terrible? Because you're not the criminal type. You have a sound sense of morality. It's not in your nature to cheat.

Or the interviewer could say almost conspiratorially:

> You didn't think there was anything wrong. The insurance company has been taking money from you for years. Everyone knows insurance companies have nothing but money. Tell me the truth now and maybe I can help.

Or in the spirit of advocacy, the interviewer could say:

> I can only get you the construction contract you need if you tell me the truth. It is impossible to find the right company unless you tell me honestly everything I need to know.

THE GUILT-BEARER

Another type of subject you may encounter is the obviously guilt-ridden person. With such a subject, you can play on his or her apparent need for forgiveness:

> You know it's wrong to take money from the account you are not entitled to, don't you? You're sorry for doing what you did. I mean, Debbie, you *are* sorry, aren't you?

Playing on a person's sense of "guilt" is an effective truth-seeking tool known to every parent, religious leader, parson, priest, imam, and rabbi. It is the feeling of guilt, more than a fear of punishment, that causes many to confess and seek forgiveness. The catharsis that comes from a confession of wrongdoing is universally felt and understood. The professional knows that playing on a sense of guilt works best with people brought up with a strict adherence to religion, or within a strong, tightly knit family.

Courts become concerned with the fairness of an interview when an interviewer inquires into a person's religious beliefs. However, such inquiries, if subtly introduced, can be a very useful tool in nonformal interviews. A chance to be absolved of a sin or a crime—to be freed of the need to continue lying—is often enough to induce a religious-minded subject to tell the whole truth. Although a fairly common method, this appeal to a sense of guilt must be used cautiously, and only by an interviewer who appears respectable and devoutly religious him- or herself.

THE JOKER OR WISE GUY

In interview situations, you will commonly encounter the "joker" or "wise guy," a personality type completely different from the guilt-bearer. He or she will act unconcerned about the seriousness of the interview and, when questioned, will try to demonstrate that he or she is too smart to fall for any interviewer's attempts to establish phony rapport. The interviewer must "sober up" this type of person or control of the interview will be lost.

Rather than ineffectively play on a morality entirely absent in the subject, the skilled interviewer must emphasize the seriousness of the situation, the punishment that potentially hangs over the subject's head, and the futility of the joker's strategy of noncooperation. The interviewer convinces the person that the chances of reward without cooperation are minuscule and that the legal consequences of a failure to cooperate are great.

A prudent and competent interviewer will firmly impress on the subject the importance of seeing the situation in a different light. The interviewer makes it clear that cooperation will be repaid with cooperation and speed, and that animosity will only be repaid with yet more animosity and delay. For example, the interviewer can use the police interrogation technique of direct accusation:

> George, this is serious. Cheating your insurance company is a crime, and you're acting like a criminal here. Do you realize that? If you keep acting like this you'll just convince the insurance company you have something to hide. If you don't cooperate you'll bring on yourself the full legal power of the insurance company. You don't want that to happen, do you?

Alternatively, if the subject responds better to less aggressive lines of questioning, a sense of endangerment can be induced by saying, for example:

> George, this is an interview to determine whether you have engaged in the very serious crime of fraud. Tell me, what do you think the appropriate punishment for insurance fraud should be?

The point is that the joker, unresponsive to appeals to morality or sense of guilt, will often respond with fear to direct or implied information about the real likelihood of serious punishment.

THE COOL CUSTOMER

The "cool customer" is neither intimidated by the interviewer nor concerned about his or her interests. This subject is neither arrogant nor entirely uncooperative, but exercises control by maintaining a genuine disinterest in the interview. Often, frustrated with this type of subject, the inexperienced interviewer will begin to express feelings that are detrimental to the interview. The frustrated interviewer is often tempted to say, "Brother, my boss must have old-timers' disease. It's affecting his mind. He's going nuts when he thinks guys like you should be given any consideration at all to get things straightened out."

Instead, the professional must impress upon the subject the seriousness of the situation and be prepared for the long session that will likely be required to wear the cool customer down.

In the next chapter, we'll take a closer look at how you can effectively get information out of subjects such as the "cool customer."

9

Approaches That Work

Some interviews are simply more difficult than others. But one thing is certain: an uncontrolled tirade never yields results. Interviewers involved in fraud investigations will often find that the frustration of dealing with the "cool customer" type may cause them to resort to a verbal outburst—a display of anger such as, "I hope you keep sticking to your damn fool story because the judge will see through it! You're a criminal and you're going to be sent away for years." Or "The only type of person I can't stand is a liar. You disgust me! Please keep on like this and I will make your life miserable." Or even more explosively, "Oh, why don't you shut up and stick to your lousy lies. I want to see you in prison for the maximum."

The abusive outburst is appealing to the frustrated interviewer because it lets his or her true feelings be heard. It may even lead to a feeling of profound catharsis. Unfortunately, however, the satisfaction that is gained is only temporary, for the outburst will completely destroy the effectiveness of the interview. The interviewer should carefully guard against and strictly avoid the temptation to indulge in such a technique, even involuntarily; in the end, it will bring the interviewer more grief than gain.

Let's now look at approaches that *do* work. Prior to an interview, the interviewer needs to select his or her approach. The adept interviewer will also select alternative approaches in the event the first choice fails.

Naturally, if a particular approach seems to be working with the person interviewed its use should be continued. Change for its own sake, or change merely to show versatility, will produce diminishing returns.

Following are some of the most effective approaches.

THE SILENT APPROACH

The interviewer enters the room with a slight smile on his or her face, sits down in the comfortable special chair, and appears confident and in control. If the person to be interviewed is standing or is sitting in the wrong chair, the interviewer just points to the chair where the subject is to sit. Expressionless, the professional looks the subject straight in the eye and says absolutely nothing.

Upon seeing the interviewer enter the room, the subject may have uttered some disparaging remark, such as, "What do you want?"; "You ain't got nothin' on me!"; "I'm a busy man, why are you keeping me waiting on this insurance matter?"; or "Why are you bothering me? Just pay the claim."

The professional shows no sign that such remarks have even registered and, once seated, looks at the subject without expression and offers no response. The person interviewed will often look away, begin to sing, or try to show unconcern in other ways.

This nonchalance is akin to the poorly feigned carefree air of the child whistling while walking through a cemetery at night. After several minutes of silence, such interviewees usually drop the pretense and will frequently then begin shifting around in their chair, crossing and recrossing their legs or arms, looking around the room, or making remarks such as, "Come off it, what do you want?"

Note that such remarks show that the subject is becoming concerned about what is going to happen. Also apparent are a noticeable trace of nervousness, a tremor in the voice where there was no such sign before the "silent treatment" began. The subject's face may develop a tic, the brow may furrow, or the tongue may constantly be wetting the lips. The person interviewed will look down at the table, across the room—anywhere to avoid the professional's insistent gaze.

This approach is much like that in the childhood game where two children stare at each other and the first to blink or look away loses the game. Here, looking away is also a sign of weakness, and in doing so the subject is already submitting to the interviewer. The silent approach will only work if the interviewer maintains direct and steady eye contact. If the interviewer is the first to waver, if the interviewer flinches or looks away, the subject wins this contest of wills.

The ancient proverb that states "the eyes are the windows of the soul" takes on added significance in this situation: guilty subjects may feel that the truth is being read, if not in their words, then through their eyes.

A subject who was self-assured and swaggering before the interview may begin to show signs of breaking and may even appear to be on the verge of tears. Succumbing to the technique, the subject may start a long narrative without being asked a single question.

If the silent treatment fails, the skilled interviewer knows from experience when to end it. When breaking the silence, a simple question can catch the subject off-guard:

> "Was it your idea, or was it Tom's?"
>
> "It was his idea; I just went along for the ride."

The silent treatment takes time. Often an interviewer is tempted to think that the tactic has failed without giving it sufficient time to take effect. Only experience (with its necessary repeated failures) will make it possible for the skilled professional to choose the right moment to break the silence.

THE FISHING APPROACH

This approach is best used when the person interviewed does not know why he or she has been called in and/or when the interviewer has little or no background information on the person to be interviewed. The interviewer starts by saying something like this:

> "I'm Mr. Legrand. You're not stupid, Marie. You certainly know why you are here, don't you?"

The subject will then guess at the reason for the interview, to which the interviewer answers:

> "Well, tell me about it, please. And remember: keep to the truth."

If the person interviewed honestly replies "No," the following dialogue may occur:

> "I'd like you to give me the story in your own words. When did you first plan it?"
>
> "I don't know what you are talking about."
>
> "Look, you know why you are here. I'd like to get your own story as to exactly what happened in your words, not in someone else's."
>
> "I still don't know what you are talking about."

"After all, lots of information we get is exaggerated. If some of this information we have about you is exaggerated, you shouldn't be blamed for a lot of things you didn't do. But until we hear from you what did happen, we just have to believe this information."

The principle behind the fishing approach is that a criminal's greatest fear concerns the most serious offense he or she has committed. If the interviewer does not give it away by overspecifying the nature of the investigation, the person being interviewed will assume that the offense in question is the most serious one.

For example, in a police matter, a man has been picked up on suspicion of stealing a car several days before. The man did, in fact commit the crime, but he is more concerned about having shot and killed a druggist several months before, during a robbery. At the time of his arrest, and until he learns differently from the police, he will probably think he is under suspicion for robbery and murder, not for the petty car theft.

When the interviewers begin to talk about car theft, the subject will immediately feel some sense of relief, believing the police are not connecting him with the robbery–murder. This gives him the confidence to be more cooperative with regard to the car theft, thinking that the police know nothing about his involvement in the more serious crime. Thus, as the police continue to fish for information, the man becomes more talkative about his activities in general, revealing information that might inadvertently lead police to suspect his connection to the murder.

Sometimes the interviewer may structure the interview to appear that a minor offense is under investigation when, in fact, the subject has been called in about a much more serious crime. Inflating values is usually a less serious crime than arson, for example, and by asking questions about minor offenses the skilled professional is actually fishing for information about a greater crime. Inquiring about travel expenditures, for example, may lead subjects to unwittingly reveal information that implicates them in embezzlement, fraud, or arson. In other words, if the interviewer doesn't state the topic of the interview, the subject will assume it concerns involvement in the "worst-crime scenario."

In the "fishing" approach, the professional listens intently and encourages the subject to reveal more by leaning forward, nodding, or just saying "uh-huh." The interviewer deals with the subject as a parent would deal with a child telling a story. By fishing, the interviewer is attempting to establish new facts, events, and connections, the details of which the subject did not know going into the interview.

The fishing approach is notorious for being potentially hazardous to interviewers if they are attorneys in a court trial and make the classic mistake of asking questions to which they do not already know the answers.

I once served as an expert witness in a case in which I was ordered, before the trial, not to testify about or use the word "arson." The attorney who cross-examined me, using the fishing approach, opened the door by using the word "arson" before the civil jury. In order to respond to his question properly, I had no choice but to also use the word "arson." Defining the nature of the case in this way had a serious impact on the ultimate verdict, and the attorney's inept attempt at fishing really backfired on him.

The fishing approach, then, should only be used as a fact-gathering tool, never in trial or before a jury, because it can reveal weaknesses in the interviewer's knowledge and can allow a jury to hear testimony detrimental to the client's best interests.

In the robbery–murder, car-theft example, the person interviewed might reply as follows to one of the interviewer's general questions about telling the truth:

"It was an accident."

The interviewer may look confused and say:

"What are you talking about?"

The interviewer will tip the subject to the fact that his or her involvement in the robbery–murder is unknown. Thus, to exploit this response to the fishing approach, the interviewer must do a great deal of quick thinking. For example, the interviewer might instead respond, "What do you mean, it was an accident! It sure didn't look that way."

"I tell you it was. I didn't mean to shoot him."

If the interviewer then asks, "When was this?" or "Who are you talking about?" or a similar question, it becomes obvious to the subject that the interviewer has little or no knowledge about the robbery–murder.

In this example, the interviewer does not know what is involved—that is, why he or she continues to ask open-ended questions. The interviewer must pick up clues as to what to say from the person interviewed. It may be more effective to say:

"What do you mean, you didn't mean to shoot him?"

The interview, in a successful fishing approach as part of a criminal investigation, may result in the following statements and questions:

"Honest, I just got panicky when he began to yell."

"You didn't really get panicky when he began to yell, did you? You've done this before."

"Sure, but I wasn't expecting the jerk to put up such a beef over fifty bucks."

"Fifty dollars? We hear it was a lot more."

"Naw, that's all he had in the register. I didn't even ask him to give me his wallet."

"That's all he had in his register, fifty dollars?"

"Yeah, and just after he handed it to me he started yelling, so I started to run out and just turned around to scare him, and the gun went off accidentally."

"And it went off accidentally? That's hard to believe. What happened next?"

"I ran right out and we drove off."

"And I imagine when you got in the car you said it was an accident."

"Yeah, I told Doug that. That I didn't mean to do it. He was madder than hell since he didn't want to get involved in anything like a shooting."

"We were told you kept all the money for yourself."

"Like hell I did! Doug got $20, I got $20 and Dave got $10."

"Again, we were told you kept all the money for yourself. If you split it three ways, where did you divide it up?"

"As soon as Dave drove in his garage, we split."

"We understand Dave was upset too."

"Yeah, he was afraid the car would be traced right to him. Say, how did you cops find out we did it?"

"Never mind how we found out, the important thing is that we found out. After you split the money, what did you do then?"

And so goes the interview, taking new directions and unraveling a story different from the expected one. The agile mind of the interviewer, listening carefully to the person interviewed, gets the whole truth without revealing that he or she did not know the facts beforehand.

Naturally, the professional is careful not to show undue interest in (or surprise at) what the subject is saying. To do so would, again, imply a lack of knowledge. In the above example, showing excitement or interest about who got the money would only have served to warn the subject to make no further admissions. The professional interviewer must endeavor to give the impression that the process of questioning is a mere formality and that he or she is calm and possesses all the pertinent details.

For example, when Doug's name was first mentioned, if the interviewer had asked, "What is Doug's last name?" the subject would have been warned that the interviewer did not know everything. The interviewer could also have concealed lack of knowledge by saying, "I want to get straight your version of what happened—it is different from our other version. I want to get it down in black and white so that no one can accuse you of lying. Now, whose idea was this?"

The interviewer then asks whose gun it was, where the gun is now, and all other pertinent details. The interviewer writes this information down in front of the witness and can thus reasonably ask for "full names, just for the record."

"Say, how does Bill spell his last name?"

"How the hell do you think he spells it? J-O-N-E-S."

The above exchange shows how an interviewer's presumed skill at the devious fishing approach can also backfire. In the above exchange, it would become immediately clear to a subject that an interviewer who pretends not to be able to spell "Jones" is fishing for information.

Fishing can be especially effective, however, if several people were complicit in a crime or know that the key subject committed a crime. Not surprisingly, when each of the confederates is interviewed privately, often each begins to feel that one or more of the others is "squealing" on them and that the safest way to escape punishment is to tell the truth.

DIRECT AND INDIRECT ACCUSATION APPROACHES

When the information gathered before the interview strongly indicates that the person interviewed is implicated in a fraudulent insurance claim, embezzlement, real estate fraud, medical fraud, or similar unlawful acts, the interviewer has a great advantage. In cases where the evidence is overwhelming, the direct accusation approach may be a shortcut to gaining the whole truth.

Distinct from a "bluff," this approach is based on absolute, established facts. It is used first to gain a quick admission and subsequently to obtain the remainder of the whole truth, which should quickly and easily follow.

Using this approach, the interviewer generally makes the accusation, directly or indirectly, at the very beginning of the interview. For example, in a robbery–murder case, a police officer might address a cool-customer type with:

> "Joe, I am Mr. O'Toole. You didn't mean to shoot that grocer, did you?"

Or, in a civil situation, the private investigator or civil attorney might start the interview with:

> "Alice, I'm Ms. Marple. You didn't intend to hurt the County of Dade when you presigned for dates on your chiropractor's record, did you?"

If the interviewer sees by the facial expressions and body language of the person interviewed that he or she is preparing a denial, the interviewer will quickly interject:

> "We know you did it. There is no question about that. I don't really think you meant to shoot him; I think that it was just an accident. It *was* an accident, wasn't it?"

Or the civil interviewer might say:

> "There is no doubt about your guilt in this matter, Alice. But I'm sure you didn't intend to hurt anyone. You just wanted to save yourself the trouble of signing in every time you came to the doctor's office, didn't you?"

The interviewer says this in an understanding and matter-of-fact tone of voice. Yet, the subject is not led to plead any noninvolvement. To catch the subject off-guard, the interviewer delivers the indirect question in a neutral tone, but at a relatively fast rate of speech. For example, the police interviewer can open the interview by saying:

- "How many other people have you shot besides that grocer last week?"
- "Besides the grocery store last week, how many other stickups have you done?"
- "How many different doctors did you go to about that one automobile accident?"
- "How many times have you made claims to Medicaid for accidents that did not happen?"

The early accusation, when delivered swiftly and in even tones, adds an element of surprise and communicates to the subject that the crime is already proven.

Responses might be:

- "That's the only time I have used a gun."
- "I just did two jobs before this robbery."
- "This was my first claim. I just did what the doctor told me to do!"
- "I've only done this twice before. No one ever complained, and the doctor always gave me half the bill. Hell, you know the insurance companies have all the money in the world."

The subject reacts defensively rather than using the logical thinking required to sustain a false story.

When dealing with a fraudulent insurance claim, a civil interviewer who is confidently armed with sufficient backup facts might say:

"Linda, you didn't mean to make a claim for the loss of a car you never owned, did you?"

"My boyfriend told me there would be no trouble. Just go to the insurance agent and buy a policy."

"You didn't have the car; how did you insure it?"

"Bill gave me a pink slip. I showed that to the agent."

Remember, the enlightened interviewer always verifies beforehand the degree and accuracy of all information available before even beginning to consider employing an accusation approach.

The direct accusation approach must be used with extreme caution and only when the facts are established with certainty.

THE BETRAYING ACCOMPLICE APPROACH

This approach, though well known to the public from television dramas, is consistently reliable and extremely effective. It is based on two principles. First, whenever two or more persons are involved in a fraud or crime, each is afraid that the other will be the one to break down and talk. Second, each is afraid that the other will betray the partnership by making a deal with the police or interviewers to escape punishment, effectively shifting all the blame to one side.

In this case, as with most of the subject's fears, the skilled interviewer exploits the subject's anxieties to his or her advantage. The approach always involves separating the two accomplices.

> Harry, you know that Tom is smart enough to know that we have you two cold on this thing. There is no question about that. And, there is no question that he's going to pin the blame on you. I'm sorry to have to tell you this, Harry, but Tom's talking and it looks like he's going to leave you holding the bag. It never fails. When we get two guys mixed up in crime, the weak one always ends up spilling everything.

Or, simply:

> "Okay, Harry, I'll give you a chance. Whose idea was it—yours or Tom's?"

A constant playing on the fear of betrayal, if done with subtle insistence, will almost always cause at least one of the conspirators to take a self-preserving position. One subject will eventually blame the other or will seek some advantage or "break" in return for information.

Naturally, in civil cases—especially when interviews take place in private homes—it may be difficult to keep the interview subjects apart. To prevent them from talking to each other, it is necessary, therefore, to have two interviewers at work. Different rooms can be requested, and separate interviews can be conducted simultaneously. While the accomplices may have previously fabricated together a credible set of lies and false alibis, physical separation prevents them from updating each other on the information revealed. It also stops them from renewing their "honor among thieves" bond of trust and from needing to assure each other that neither will submit and confess nor resort to betrayal.

It is an interesting aspect of human nature that the person interviewed will often take a cue from the interviewer and throw all the blame on the partner. Occasionally, the interviewer will get confessions from two persons in which both admit participating in the crime. Each puts all the blame on the other and will claim that the other did the deed or committed the fraud.

In *State Farm Fire & Cas. Co. v. Tan*, 691 F. Supp. 1271 Sept. 1, 1988), the United States District Court found that "separate examinations could lead to a recount of facts as the individual insured remembers them, and circumvents [sic] the possibility that the insured's recollection of events will be subconsciously altered because of suggestion from prior testimony." In so many words, the federal courts have approved the sequestering of witnesses to allow interviewers to obtain more accurate information.

In *Ahmadi v. Allstate Insurance Co.*, 22 P.3d 576 (Colo. App. Mar. 15, 2001), however, the Colorado Court of Appeals refused sequestration without a requirement that the claimant appear for examination under oath outside the presence of other claimants. In short, a civil interviewer should determine how the law applies in the state where the interview is to take place.

Often, if asked politely, the two accomplices will allow the interviewer to speak to each privately. If the interviewer does not have a contractual ability to separate them, as did State Farm in the *Tan* case, courtesy often works to get a voluntary separation.

THE INCOMPETENCE APPROACH

If the evidence of fraud indicates that poor planning and clumsy execution brought the fraud to the insurer's attention, the interviewer can mock the subject's competence with comments such as:

- "I have heard how intelligently you have worked in the past. How could someone like you make an obvious mistake that even a 10-year-old kid wouldn't make?"

- "You left a gas can with the price tag on it in the building."
- "You kept the 'stolen' encyclopedia at your brother's house."
- "You left the files in the trunk of a rented car!"

Although the incompetence approach is often effective with the nervous subject who is already lacking in self-confidence, the interviewer should never use it without detailed facts derived from independent investigation.

THE APPEAL TO PRIDE APPROACH

This approach is the inverse of the incompetence approach. It plays on the subject's criminal arrogance. The subject's pride in his or her skills can be exploited to the interviewer's advantage. In order to get any recognition for outwitting an insurance company, a governmental agency, or a big business concern, the egotistical subject must talk to claim credit. The interviewer might say:

> "You know, I've been around a long time. This is one of the smartest operations I have ever seen. This was a brilliantly executed scheme. Not your run-of-the-mill insurance scam. You've got to admire the intelligence of any person who could pull this one off."

Or

> "It took intelligence and training to figure this one out. When did you first get the idea?"

Or

> "This was sure a smooth operation. I've seen lots of men try to accomplish this, but they always mess it up. This was really done with finesse. Who else but a clever guy like you could have pulled it off? When did you first decide to do it?"

The interviewer could flatter the subject as if he or she were a member of MENSA, the famous society open only to people who score at the 98th percentile or higher on a standardized IQ test. This approach is especially effective when interviewing a person who is uneducated, looked down upon by acquaintances, and in need of some hard-earned praise. The interview is possibly this person's very first chance to show anyone that he or she is intelligent. In the short term, the prospect of being acclaimed as the brilliant person who conceived and carried out the crime outweighs the ignominy of criminal conviction or the loss of a civil suit.

THE DEGRADING APPROACH

This approach is also used on the egotistical person, especially when the interviewer is certain that the person was the principal instigator of a particular crime. The difference is that this approach attempts to get information by dismissing or downgrading the subject's importance.

> "Ralph, who put you up to doing this? It is pretty obvious that someone told you how to do it. I'm sure you couldn't have figured the complexities of the insurance policy and claim process out yourself. Now, who told you?"

If others are involved, the interviewer might say:

> "It is obvious that you are the stupid one in this deal. I'm sure you were used as the fall guy for the 'brains' behind this operation. Certainly, you never figured this out for yourself. I'll bet it was you who made the mistake that led us right to you. Someone else had to have told you how to collect food stamps under 15 different names. Who was it?"

Or

> "This was a really sophisticated scam. Somebody obtained medical provider numbers from legitimate doctors and set up businesses using those numbers to defraud Medicare. But this type of detail is beyond your ability. Who told you what to do?"

Keeping up this approach may so enrage subjects that they can often make damaging admissions to prove they weren't just the "stupid slobs" in the operation.

THE "WE ALL MAKE MISTAKES" APPROACH

By projecting an attitude of understanding, even compassion, the interviewer can remove the subject's concern for concealing the truth.

The interviewer using this approach may say:

> "We all make foolish mistakes. I know I certainly have. None of us is perfect."

Or

> "People make mistakes all the time when presenting claims to insurance companies. It doesn't necessarily mean they intended to commit fraud, right? Tell me what happened in this case."

Or

> "It's not a big deal. I can see how you would have decided to do as you did. Let's just get the facts straight and then you can go, okay?"

By downplaying the seriousness of the offense and appearing to identify with the subject, the interviewer can get at the truth. The interviewer may even show some antagonism in the complicit approach, albeit directed toward mutual enemies: judges, juries, bosses, or corporations.

THE AMUSED APPROACH

Nobody likes to be laughed at. Laughing at egotistical or cool-customer types usually upsets them more than anything. Giving off an air of amused condescension throughout, the interviewer may say:

> "Your story is the funniest I have heard in years! Boy, seldom do we have such an open-and-shut case. With all the evidence we've got, it's really a joke that you believe you're going to profit from this phony claim."

Or

> "Why, last week it took only four minutes for a jury to come back with a verdict in favor of the insurance company. They even assessed damages! And they only had about one-third of the evidence we have on you. If it weren't so damned funny, it would be pathetic."

Or

> "That's hilarious, George. You want the insurance company to pay you a million bucks for the trouble *you*'ve caused!"

The interviewer using this approach must be extremely practiced at conveying a mood of amusement, as laughter that is not rooted in real feeling (and gestures that are too theatrical) will be unconvincing to the subject.

Frauds and other people who want to keep secrets are very quick to detect falsity in the interviewer. The best way to use this approach is to find something genuinely laughable in the subject's amateurish attempts to deceive.

The approaches suggested here should not constrain interviewers. Professionals should only use as guidelines the approaches they can modify or combine with their own creative improvisations. They should experiment constantly to find which approaches work best.

10

Dealing with the Nervous Person

When investigating fraud or other white-collar crime, the professional knows how to exploit the subject's fear of being caught in an illegal act of deception and of suffering punishment. Obviously, how much fear a person feels at the time of the interview depends on the person's personal background and psychological makeup. But the time that has elapsed between the actual commission of a crime and any investigative interview can be of equal importance.

The subject, knowing that the professional has been actively compiling background information, will often enter the interview with an acutely heightened sense of fear. Many find it impossible to hide the obvious signs of this accumulated fear. These are the "nervous persons," as distinct from the "cool customers" discussed in the last chapter.

The nervous person tries hard to control the outward signs of nervousness by concentrating on restraining emotion. Sometimes, to mask or reduce stress, this type of subject will resort to taking drugs. The interviewer should, therefore, always question the person interviewed about possible drug use, whether that involves prescription medicines or illegal drugs. The interviewer should note the following signs of nervousness carefully:

- dry skin.
- dilated pupils.
- cold, clammy hands.

- signs of fever.
- perspiration.
- unseasonable excess of clothing.
- cracked, wavering, or high-pitched voice.
- constant lip-licking.
- habitual foot-tapping or leg-shaking.
- eye twitching or abnormal frequency of blinking.
- cupping of the forehead in both hands.
- strained facial muscles.
- loosening a necktie or unbuttoning a shirt.
- beads of perspiration at the hairline or on the upper lip.
- skin discoloration.

The unobservant, unskilled interviewer will sometimes miss these signs, enabling the subject to successfully mask nervousness.

The key to a successful interview is the interviewer's interest in observing the subject of the interview and listening to what the subject has to say. Taking notes on what is said or looking down at a prepared list of questions defeats the ability to take direction from the subject's reaction to the interview.

BEHAVIOR PATTERNS

Everyone displays behavior patterns. Unfortunately for the professional interviewer, the behavior patterns of a nervous, guilty person can be identical to those exhibited by an honest, innocent person who is simply more prone to stress. It is the duty of the professional to analyze any given subject type's physical signs, statements, and behavior patterns and how they combine to indicate that the subject is lying.

The professional recognizes that some people are nervous in *every* social situation, especially those that are formal or have criminal implications. Evidence of nervousness alone is not proof that a person is lying, as many people can be nervous even when actually telling the truth.

If, however, a subject is calm throughout an interview and then suddenly manifests the behavior patterns discussed below, there is a strong probability that the person interviewed is not being truthful, at least with regard to a particular point. If, conversely, the person interviewed is nervous throughout the interview, the behaviors below may mean nothing. For fun—but fun of the most instructional variety—let's look at outlines of a number of behavior types.

The Sartorially Obsessed

This subject, perhaps suffering from burdensome pangs of conscience, signals nervousness by way of an exaggerated concern for appearance. The subject will:

- avoid the interviewer's gaze by studying his or her own clothing minutely;
- pretend to find lint or other nonexistent debris on clothing;
- repeatedly and unnecessarily straighten clothing; or
- be unusually concerned with hair and general neatness.

The Gulper

Fear and nervousness can affect the subject's autonomic nervous system, involuntarily signaling such nervousness by:

- repeatedly swallowing saliva, so that the Adam's apple bounces up and down like a basketball; or
- continually wiping the mouth with a handkerchief.

The Person with an Insatiable Thirst

When the interviewer encounters this behavior in a subject, offering a glass of water can produce results. However, the subject, upon receiving water, may simply try to employ the glass as a kind of prop in an effort to avoid the interviewer's questions. This subject exhibits the following behaviors:

- "dry mouth";
- continuous licking of the lips or rotation of the tongue;
- repeated requests for water;
- speaking in a hoarse voice;
- apparent difficulty with the simple mechanics of speech; or
- need to continuously chew gum or suck on candy.

The Muscle-Spasm Sufferer

Some subjects unconsciously move their fingers, toes, hands, or feet. For that reason, as stated before, it is useful for the interviewer to be in close proximity to the person interviewed. The professional always notes the following types of nervous activity:

- leg crossing and re-crossing.
- incessant foot-tapping.
- rapid leg-bouncing.
- repeated finger-tapping.

The Fidgeter

This subject moves around so much that he or she seems to be seated on a red ant mound rather than a chair. Fidgeting most often begins immediately after a subject is asked an important question. Fidgeting includes:

- constant changes of seating position and posture.
- scratching or rubbing of body parts.
- evident desire to stand up.
- general inability to control body movement.

The Statue

When confronted by a professional interviewer, some subjects turn into statues, like Lot's wife who, despite strong admonitions not to look back at the destruction of Sodom and Gomorrah, was turned into a pillar of salt. Statues can be easily spotted since they:

- sit bolt-upright in a chair as if glued into position;
- demonstrate no signs of emotion;
- fold and lock their legs and/or arms;
- speak in a monotone, if at all;
- use their hands to cover or partially block the mouth;
- never change position regardless of how long the interview lasts; or
- stare off into space and do not look at the interviewer.

The Amnesiac

This type has decided that covering up lies or keeping lies consistent is going to be an exhausting and quite possibly a futile exercise. The subject will choose to "forget" details and will exhibit some physical behaviors that will signal, to an astute interviewer, an attempt at deceit. The subject feigning amnesia will often:

- appear dazed or unreasonably tired;
- take 5 to 10 seconds to respond to questions;
- maintain a blank stare; or
- limit responses to "I don't remember."

By weighing what information has been "forgotten" and noting what (if any) information the subject was willing to divulge, the interviewer can better determine whether the subject is truly under such stress that genuine amnesia is at work or whether the subject is just feigning an inability to recollect.

NERVOUSNESS, THE FALSE POSITIVE

The prudent interviewer recognizes that indications of nervousness may have nothing to do with guilt or innocence, nor necessarily signal that a subject is attempting to hide the truth. Circumstances serious enough to require an interview by a professional are quite enough to make most people nervous.

Medical doctors are faced with a similar problem: the phenomenon of the "White Coat Syndrome." For example, it has been observed that a person will register a higher blood pressure when it is taken by a doctor in a white coat than when it is taken in the home by a spouse. The fear of being found sick increases in the presence of a doctor, and this fear will act to give a false positive for high blood pressure. Aware of this prevalent syndrome, doctors will take the patient's blood pressure on both arms, allowing the patient time to relax between tests.

The professional interviewer recognizes that the fact of the interview alone is enough to transform some normally calm persons into nervous wrecks. The novice interviewer, however, may read the false positive of nervousness as proof of guilt or prevarication.

The experienced interviewer is always aware that both innocent and guilty subjects can show signs of general, even extreme, nervousness.

However, the learned professional also knows one thing more: such nervousness in innocent subjects will abate at some time after the process has begun and the interviewer has established rapport. The guilty person's nervous signals will likely proliferate throughout the interview. The interviewer must nonetheless recognize that the exact opposite can be true, depending on the personality of the person interviewed. Certainty only comes to the interviewer with experience and obtaining corroborating evidence.

In any case, no one possesses a perfect memory. And when, in the course of an investigation, a subject is called upon to remember extremely unpleasant details, he or she can have a genuine traumatic reaction, causing the mind to subconsciously refuse to allow the incident to be brought forward to consciousness.

On the other hand, if the lack of recollection is based on spurious claims, the professional cannot accept the claim of amnesia without pursuing the matter further.

The subject may say:

> "I blacked out."

Or

> "I was too drunk to remember."

The prudent interviewer will give credence to such statements only if corroborating facts have been obtained by investigation or from other reliable sources.

"NERVOUS" STATEMENTS TO WATCH OUT FOR

Often, people who lie try too hard to convince the interviewer of their truthfulness. Indicators of falsehood can be recognized when the person interviewed uses, insistently or repeatedly, the following expressions:

- "To tell the truth . . ."
- "To be perfectly frank . . ."
- "Honestly . . ."
- "On my mother's grave . . ."

- "I never lie . . ."
- "I swear . . ."

Let's look in detail at some more types of statements that can tip the interviewer off that the subject is lying.

"My Blood Pressure Medicine Affects My Memory"

This person may have used the simple "I can't remember" ploy too often and has decided to resort to a more credible excuse based on personal medical history. The prudent interviewer will always require the subject to provide details of any medication taken, including the dosage, and will ask for medical records or contact the subject's physician.

- "I need my medication."
- "The doctor says my anxiety pills are affecting my memory."
- "I have mild schizophrenia."
- "I am clinically depressed."
- "I am bipolar."

The subject may indeed have been prescribed medicine that might affect recall, but the professional will be alert to a possible avoidance strategy and will certainly not automatically accept that no information can be gained. The professional will ask to view and copy the subject's medication bottle for the prescription and the actual name of the drug, and will also request a report from the subject's physician to corroborate the claim. The *Physician's Desk Reference* and various websites can help the interviewer verify the drug's side effects.

"What Would My Family Think of Me?"

This type of statement indicates the type of nervous person who seems more concerned with family image, social standing, or reputation than with failure to cooperate in any interview. The professional can work on this very common fear of social disgrace but must do so with caution and great care. The delicate operation involves the interviewer assuming a role similar to that of a family member and convincing the subject that the loving family will be entirely forgiving after the whole truth is revealed. In an effort to suggest that he or she could not possibly be involved in such a crime or wrongdoing, a subject might say things like:

- "My wife would leave me if I ever did anything like that."
- "I'd never do such a thing. It would break my mother's heart."
- "My family thinks I'm a big success in the Big Apple."

"Who, Me?"

This kind of response indicates that the subject is attempting to gain time or avoid direct answers by volleying meaningless questions back at the interviewer or by giving vague responses.

Variations include the following:

- "It could be said so."
- "Could you please rephrase that question?"
- "As I understand your question, yes."
- "As I understand your question, no."
- "That has no relevance to my claim."
- "It depends on the meaning of 'yes.'"
- "Why are you trying to invade my privacy?"

None of these variations give the interviewer any information, but they all buy the subject time. Responses of this kind call for additional, immediate, direct questioning. The interviewer should always consider them to be merely rhetorical ploys and should not fall into the trap of answering them.

"I Was Brought Up Strictly; I Would Never Lie"

This kind of statement may alert the interviewer to the possibility that the subject person is trying to hide behind a veneer of respectability. He or she presents quite a show of being outraged and insulted. This subject protests too much and acts seriously offended that his or her character should even be challenged. Such a response must always be taken with a healthy dose of skepticism.

Variations on the theme include:

- "I am a devout Christian."
- "I'm a pillar of my community."

- "I'm a military man."
- "I'm a philosopher."
- "I am an honorable man."
- "I'm a Sunday School teacher."
- "I'm a minister."
- "I'm not a bullshit artist."
- "I cannot tell a lie."
- "Why would *I* do such a thing?"

The subject tries to use the power of wealth, social standing, or political status, or other claims of presumed respectability, to defuse the interview.

While many have succeeded in hiding behind such tactics, recent news of $50 billion Ponzi schemes run by "pillars of the community" and fraud cases involving well-respected attorneys and members of Congress teach us that such rhetorical protestations are, of themselves, unconvincing.

COUNTER-RESPONSES FOR INTERVIEWERS

Earlier I stressed that the interview is a lengthy process involving shifts in control, information flow, and tempo that call upon the professional's resourcefulness and skill in rapidly adapting to any situation. When subjects use the ploys cited above, the agility of the true professional immediately comes into play to recognize the ploy and defeat it by intelligent, effective interviewing.

The "You Have a Motive" Response

A subject may invoke his or her status or wealth as being self-evident proof of innocence and should make clear that any suggestion of responsibility or criminal involvement is preposterous. This bluff is easily circumvented. The professional does not take such comments as proof of anything and always has counter-responses ready and waiting.

If the person interviewed says, for example:

> "I make $200,000 a year. Why would I make a false claim on a $20,000 car?"

The interviewer can answer:

> "Sam, there's not a person in this world who doesn't need more money. With the high cost of things today, and taxes going up, your $200,000 a year is nothing."

Or, if the interviewer's preinterview research resulted in the availability of important information, the interviewer can come back with:

> "Bill, you make a lot of money, but you *spend* even more. You didn't have the cash to pay your taxes last April, did you?"

The counter-response is effective because it weakens the resolve of the person interviewed, who had hoped the interviewer would be cowed by references to money or implied social rank. Once the professional shows the subject that the bluff has been called, the subject's façade is destroyed.

The Shared-Faith Response

The more common ground the interviewer establishes between him- or herself and the subject, the more the likelihood of getting the truth increases. Religion is by nature something people are liable to have in common. While the interviewer and the subject may not be followers of precisely the same religion, the tenets of the major world religions are all but universal.

Sincere adherents of any religion have a deeply felt sense of right and wrong. The interviewer must therefore be a constant student of the humanities, familiar with the basic principles and beliefs of every religion that might be practiced in the area where he or she works. In my massive hometown of multicultural Los Angeles, for example, that means virtually every religion practiced in the world, from Animism to Zoroastrianism.

The professional, by necessity an expert in the field of comparative religion, will use this knowledge of the subject's moral beliefs to uncover the truth. When an interviewer can converse intelligently with a subject about religion, showing honest respect for the belief system involved, a clear rapport will develop between them.

Then, when confronted with a religious defense like the ones cited above, the interviewer will be able to make an informed appeal to the subject's sensitivity to the moral code of his or her chosen faith. For example, when dealing with a subject belonging to one of the religious groups in the Judeo-Christian tradition, the notion of the fear of God (and the concept of Hell) can be a powerful aid to obtain the truth.

The "You Remind Me of My Brother" Response

Equal to—or perhaps even surpassing—religious allegiance as a potential tool for getting the truth from a subject is the human experience of family, with all its attendant joys and rewards, problems and pressures.

A 50-year-old female subject may be pleased to be compared with the interviewer's 25-year-old sister. A 50-year-old man will likely be flattered by a comparison with the interviewer's 35-year-old brother.

The interviewer is not just using flattery here; the professional is implying, and simultaneously building, a kind of kinship (albeit artificial) that can lead to greater trust and sharing:

> "If my little brother were sitting in that chair, I know he would tell me the truth."

To the subject who denies all possible involvement in any wrongdoing because his or her family values are so strong as to guarantee innocence, the interviewer will similarly appeal to those very values. The need for family support, continuity, and, ultimately, forgiveness is usually stronger than the burden of carrying and concealing a shame.

> "Family is everything to me, too, John. I know how you feel, believe me. So, yes, please do think of your wife and children. Only by telling the truth can you ever hope to keep their love and respect."

In this manner, the skilled interviewer turns back, onto the subject, the same appeal to family values and transforms it into a real option that the subject may then choose to take.

The "I Would Probably Have Done the Same Thing" Response

It's a curious thing that a subject will almost always eagerly accept any expression of understanding from an interviewer. If the interviewer's comments serve not to vilify the subject, but rather appear to almost justify his or her actions, the subject feels a closer identification with the interviewer.

Professionals can convey the sense that they, too, under similar circumstances, might have been tempted to commit the particular offense under investigation. The subject, hearing such personal identification from the interviewer, is then far more likely to tell a totally truthful and detailed story. This approach may work well with the false amnesiac, the silent "statue" type, the family person, or the religious person.

Most people enjoy receiving compliments and approval, and they react negatively to constant criticism and disapproval. When, at a family gathering, Uncle Bill disagrees about everything from the flavor of the turkey dinner to the latest statement by the local mayor, he soon finds himself alone in a corner drinking beer and eating the last of the popcorn.

People who habitually adopt a contrary attitude are eventually ostracized from their social group. But if Uncle Bill could learn to be understanding about different tastes and political stripes, people might be more willing to engage him in conversation. The same is true of the interviewer–subject relationship. For example, a man suspected of presenting a fraudulent burglary claim by adding to the list a few valuable items he never actually owned could be approached as follows:

"Bill, I understand this is your first insurance claim in 30 years of buying insurance."

"Yeah."

"You are a good customer. I see you have been insured with this company for 10 years."

"I saw no reason to change."

"You must have paid thousands of dollars to the company over the years."

"For the last few years I thought I was just dumping the money down the toilet, but now I'm glad I had the insurance. This burglary has been traumatic for my wife and me."

"I bet you're upset that I'm taking all this time with you, such a good customer, presenting your first claim."

"No, I understand."

"I'd be upset. In fact, I'd be so upset after all that money I put into the company that I'd try to get some of my money back."

"Well, that's what I've been paying for all these years."

"Bill, you know you're entitled to recover for what you lost but not for what you didn't lose, no matter how much you paid to the company."

"I know that. That's what I'm claiming."

"All I really want to know is what you really lost, Bill, so I can get the money to you."

"I appreciate your help. Ask me what you need to know."

"Then tell me, Bill, why are you making claim for this 52-inch plasma television set that you say was in this corner of the living room? You and I both know such a large set wouldn't fit there. I think what happened, Bill, is that you felt . . . just as I do . . . that you had paid premium after premium for nothing, and you just decided it was time to get some of it back. You didn't believe it would hurt an insurance company that has thousands of your dollars. That was it, wasn't it? You didn't really consider it stealing, did you?"

This openly understanding response will work occasionally, especially if the subject assumes (although not from any statement by the interviewer) that the value of the nonexistent TV will be merely deducted from the claim. Most people are unaware that a small fraud on an insurance claim defeats the entire claim. A person cannot commit a little fraud any more than he or she could just be a little dead.

If, at any moment in the interview, the subject becomes aware that admitting to even the smallest instance of fraud will deprive him or her of the entire claim, he or she will admit nothing. Standard insurance policies provide that if the insured commits fraud of any degree, the entire policy is voided. A policy would be declared void for a $400 fraud as quickly and effectively as for a $400,000 fraud.

The "Lots of People Have Done What You Did" Response

This response, almost identical to the last example, attempts to assure the subject that what he or she has done is neither unusual nor particularly serious or important.

"Stephanie, you've heard on television about how insurance fraud is everywhere, haven't you? Insurance companies include in the premium they charge the money they know will be taken by fraud. It is so common that some people believe that at least 50% of all insurance claims are fraudulent. Most people in the country don't think there is anything wrong with taking money from an insurance company."

"I've heard that."

"I can understand how people feel when they make an insurance claim. They need the money, and they think there's really nothing wrong with taking money from an insurance company that has been taking money from them for years."

You know, Stephanie, I know for a fact that lots of people have done what you did. After all, how much can a human being tolerate? How much can an insurance company take from you before you get some of it back?

After such a response, knowing that the interviewer considers the offense to be a minor one, the subject may begin to reveal the salient details and allow the whole truth to unfold.

The "Be a Man" Response

Young men are often raised to be strong, and not to be afraid of doing what is right for themselves, their group, or their family. The Spanish term for this, *macho,* has long since entered into common English usage. Calling upon this ingrained sense of pride, the interviewer can challenge the subject to prove his "manliness" by speaking honestly.

The wise guy, the silent type, and others may be addressed, for example, with something along the lines of:

"Albert, you know lying takes no guts at all. Anyone can lie. But it takes a real man to tell the truth. Are you a real man, Albert? Do you have the guts to tell the truth?"

Or

"Sandy, I don't think you are a coward. Your dad brought you up to be an upstanding citizen . . . to be brave just like he is, didn't he? How do you think he'd feel if he knew you were backing down from the truth and lying to me here?"

These are but a few examples of the counter-responses experienced professionals can make. Reading the subject type and listening carefully for the nuances of the subject's answers, behaviors, and defenses, the professional interviewers use all these skills and more to their advantage as the interview unfolds.

11

Bluffs

A "bluff" is a statement made by an interviewer indicating that certain details are already known and established, whereas, in fact, they have neither been proven to be true nor admitted as being such by the subject. Another ploy of misdirection, often catching the subject off-guard, the bluff is a technique interviewers often find effective.

Rather than ask the subject whether such and such a detail is true, the interviewer can casually propose that the critical bit of information is a given. The subject, sensing the futility of denial, may choose to elaborate or qualify the point with further information.

But be warned: the fastest way to end an interview is to use a poorly thought-out or "wild guess" bluff. In fact, we will see that in civil cases, even the best-laid bluff should be used only as a last resort. The subject, knowing the facts and perceiving that the interviewer does not, can easily call the interviewer's bluff. All of the interviewer's hard work will be undermined by the exposed bluff, and the interview will end abruptly.

For example, an interviewer might say:

"I have an eyewitness who saw you set the fire."

Or

"I know you never owned that flat-screen television. Why don't you drop your claim?"

Or

"I have your fingerprints on the window of the house where the burglary occurred."

Subjects who are not guilty of the allegations have nothing to hide. They do not hesitate to call the interviewer's bluff and reply, "Oh yeah? Bring him in and let me hear *him* say I'm involved!" or "Show me the proof!" In this cat-and-mouse game, the interviewer might deduce from such statements that the subject is telling the truth. Only the guilty subject skilled in the counterbluff would be likely to employ such ready denial.

If a bluff is called, however, and the interviewer cannot produce the proof or the eyewitness, credibility and trust can and will be damaged. Therefore, the bluff must only be used when substantial cumulative evidence points to a highly probable conclusion.

INFERENCES AND IMPLICATIONS

A more subtle form of the bluff is the mere implication that certain points are factual. For example, investigating a case of suspected arson involving a private residence, you establish that, several hours before the fire, the owner bought 10 gallons of gasoline in cans. The firefighters reported that gasoline was found in all parts of the house and that the kitchen suffered the greatest damage. From such known facts you may infer that the fire was started in the kitchen.

The homeowner, with financial gain as a motive, is the prime suspect being interviewed. The unskilled interviewer may be tempted to overdo the bluff by saying:

> "Sam, you bought 10 gallons of gas at Joe's Gas Station. You had Joe put it in two five-gallon cans; then you brought it home and poured it throughout all the rooms of your house. You then started the fire in the kitchen. We know it and we can prove it."

If the subject realizes that the interviewer knows the basic facts, he or she will feel that the facts themselves imply guilt. Therefore, a more effective approach may be to say:

> "Sam, on the day before the fire you bought 10 gallons of gas at Joe's Gas Station. We have the cash register receipts and security cam footage. The gas was in two five-gallon cans. After the fire we found two five-gallon cans stamped with Joe's logo in the kitchen of your house. Isn't it true you carried those cans into the house?"

Confronted with this approach, the subject is led to infer that the interviewer may possess even more information, as yet not divulged. He or she knows that the two cans of gasoline must be accounted for and that an implication of guilt is skillfully being presented.

By sticking to the known facts and by not risking any unsubstantiated bluff, the interviewer implies rather than accuses, allowing the nervous subject to supply the missing details.

KEEP IT SIMPLE

If the interviewer is to use the bluff as an interview technique, it must be kept as simple as possible. The bluff does not always require an accusation or overt assertion of facts. Its value is enhanced by the commonly held belief that all big corporations, especially insurers, have unlimited funds with which to conduct investigations. It is important that the interviewer exploit this misconception by revealing the minimum of information while simultaneously implying comprehensive knowledge.

Using this method, the interviewer succeeds in the bluff by causing the subject to *infer* what the well-presented facts so obviously *imply*. Often the most effective question is not a question at all. The best bluffs are implied, not stated.

DON'T BLUFF WITHOUT SOME FACTUAL SUPPORT

Outright bluffs are dangerous in civil investigations. The professional never uses the ploy at the start of an investigation. In any case, if you are considering using the bluff, always measure the small possibility of gain against the likelihood of failure.

The professional knows that for a bluff to work, these elements must be in place:

- The bluff must be delivered at a time when the person interviewed is uncomfortable.
- The subject must be deprived of contact with family, friends, and other sources of support.
- The bluff must be logical and credible.
- The subject must have already inferred that the interviewer knows more than he or she is revealing.

Bluffs work best in police interviews, where the power of the badge is in effect. In civil cases, only when all other techniques have failed should the bluff technique be tried at all. The subject will call upon the interviewer to prove the truth of all the assertions he or she makes.

At the very least, an ill-executed bluff will be an embarrassing setback for the interviewer. At worst, it will be difficult to explain in court if the subject sues, alleging that deception was involved. The subject may trot it out before the jury as evidence of the tortious conduct and the bad faith of the principal for whom the interviewer is working.

THE THREATENING BLUFF

In *Simpson v. Jackson*, 615 F.3d 421 (6th Cir. 2010) the United States Sixth Circuit Court of Appeals repeated the following from a police interview:

> This is your opportunity [to provide information about a case of arson]. 'Cause if not, you're going down with [the accused, Kelly], and guess what? Being an accomplice carries the same penalty as the person that threw the bottle. We've proven to you that we don't play games. We don't bluff.

The officers also stated:

> You are not the focus of our investigation. But if we leave this room tonight with no answers, you will be. You are looking at the rest of your life, possibly the death [penalty]—death row. If that's the game you want to play, Peanut, we'll take you there.

The police officers in this case employed threatening bluffs on a suspect whom they had arrested before, a suspect who was familiar with such strategies. The bluffs, however, were relatively unsuccessful because they rendered some of the statements made by the suspect inadmissible in court.

BLUFFING: ALWAYS A LAST RESORT

We have seen that, although it can be a useful tool when wielded sparingly, the bluff carries with it inherent risks. Even the professional draws on it only when he or she has exhausted all other routes to getting the whole truth.

12

The Interview

HOW LONG SHOULD AN INTERVIEW LAST?

Three main factors determine how long an interview should last: the physical and mental condition of the subject; the seriousness of the investigation; and the subject's reaction to the interviewing process.

Physical Condition of the Subject

Provided that the subject is healthy and in reasonable physical condition, the interview can last several hours without the interviewer receiving any undue criticism. This is especially true if the interviewer undergoes the same conditions as the person interviewed. In most cases, if the interviewer leaves the room to get a drink, eat some food, or go to the toilet, the subject should be given the opportunity to do likewise.

Before beginning, the careful interviewer makes sure that the subject has no physical needs. Then, if during the interview the subject asks for a drink of water, the interviewer can reply:

> "Janice, remember, just before we started here I asked you if you wanted a drink. You said 'yes' and you had a full glass. Now you want another drink.
>
> "Really, you could drink a lake full of water and still be thirsty because you are not telling the truth. The only drink that will make you feel good is your telling the truth. Now I'm convinced you are concealing information."

Or the interviewer might say:

> "Lyle, should I be concerned about your health? It seems to me this need for water is an indication of illness. Dry mouth in a simple conversation like this is either an indication of diabetes or drug use, or evidence that you are untruthful."

Naturally, if the person interviewed is in poor physical health, the interview should be of shorter duration. For example, all other things being equal, the interviewer would not want to interview a 92-year-old person in poor health as long as a 32-year-old in good health. To get the whole truth from the older person, you may need to interview the subject over a period of several days.

If the interviewer has definite proof that the subject has an extremely serious physical defect, such as a bad heart, it would be very wise to have a doctor present. Such a precaution, though uncommon, serves to protect the interviewer from any charges of abuse that could later arise. I once had a court order a witness—who was ill—to testify, but his doctor had to be present and had the right to stop the interview. I asked the subject's name, received an answer, and the doctor stopped the interview. Surely, time wasted!

Topic of the Inquiry

The second factor in determining how long an interview should last is, of course, the seriousness of the matter under investigation. Investigators will spend more time interviewing a person suspected of setting an arson fire than a person who falsely claimed the theft of an insured bicycle. The operator of a steel mill that employs hundreds of workers will undergo greater scrutiny than the proprietor of a small dress shop. And the owner of a jewelry store with a $2 million inventory will find her application for insurance more heavily vetted than that of the owner of a store specializing in secondhand clothing.

The Subject's Reaction

The third factor that guides interview duration—how the person being interviewed is reacting to the process—is extremely important. With experience, an alert interviewer can accurately determine the effect the various approaches and strategies are having on the subject.

If a conscientious interviewer has exhausted his or her repertoire of techniques and sees that none of them is working, it is usually best to end the interview as soon as possible. The interviewer returns to conducting other forms of investigation, after which he or she may choose to schedule another interview with the subject.

If, on the other hand, the interviewer perceives that one or more approaches are having a noticeable effect on the subject, he or she will extend the interview.

By extending the interview, the subject is given the subliminal message that the information volunteered so far is considered inadequate. Many interviewers routinely extend an interview for an additional 10 to 15 minutes beyond the estimate that was given to the subject at the start. The reasoning behind this extension is that the subject is usually under much more strain and fatigue than is the interviewer. The professional always considers the subject more compelled to break down and tell the truth than he or she is to quit.

13

The Mutability of Memory

Now that we've become familiar with the interview process and have learned techniques to use at various stages in order to get the whole truth, it is important to spend a couple of chapters examining how memory influences the information you obtain. Few people have a perfect eidetic (photographic) memory. Memory is a fluid and often unreliable human function.

During my time as a trainee investigator at the Army Intelligence School at Fort Holabird, Maryland, a classroom lecture on interviewing was interrupted by a man dressed in a clown mask, a tuxedo, swim fins, a cowboy hat, and a purple cummerbund. He ran into the room, screamed epithets, fired a weapon into the ceiling, and ran out. The teacher instructed each member of the class to write down a description of the intruder. None of our descriptions were accurate, and we were all shocked when the shooter was brought back into the class. The noise he made, the firing of a weapon, and the fear the incident engendered made it almost impossible to recall him accurately. Some even described him as having been female.

The professional recognizes that some interview techniques can cause honest subjects—those who are innocent but are "just trying to be helpful"—to "misremember" and provide unreliable, even false, information. It has long been known that false memories can be implanted through suggestion, especially when used by skillful but unscrupulous attorneys or interviewers.

Leading questions—whose desired answers are suggested by the way the question is phrased—are a dangerous impediment to fact finding.

The true professional, impartial and seeking only the truth, must guard against even inadvertently leading a subject to creating false memories.

LIES AND MEMORY

Use of a suggestive interview technique can be material to preparation of the defense, and the courts have recognized that suggestive interview techniques are material to the credibility of prosecution witnesses.

In *Jenkins v. Com.*, 308 SW 3d 704 (Ky. 2010), the Kentucky Supreme Court noted that similar to expert testimony involving eyewitness identification, expert testimony that a witness was subjected to suggestive interview techniques pertains to the reliability or accuracy of the witness's belief or recollection, not to the truthfulness or untruthfulness of the witness. [Compare *Commonwealth v. Christie,* 98 S.W.3d 485 (Ky. 2002) (expert eyewitness identification testimony).] To the contrary, such evidence assumes that the witness is testifying truthfully but may be mistaken in his or her belief. Accordingly, the trial court erred in ruling that the evidence was inadmissible as a matter of law and the case was remanded to the trial court for trial, with the expert allowed to testify.

In *People v. Zwart,* 600 N.E.2d 1169, 151 Ill.2d 37, 175 Ill.Dec. 711 (Ill. 1992), the Supreme Court of Illinois recognized the problem with suggestive interviewing techniques, as follows:

> Evidence as to what transpired during these interviews was particularly important here for two reasons. First, the victim's age made her particularly susceptible to suggestion from outsiders. Second, the defendant was unable to question the victim about the interviews at trial because the trial court found the victim incompetent to testify. A trial court should not presume from a silent record that suggestive interview techniques were not used. Careful consideration of the circumstances surrounding the victim's statements is particularly important in cases such as this, where the defendant does not have the opportunity to cross-examine the victim. The State, as the proponent of the challenged statements, bore the burden of establishing that the statements were reliable and not the result of adult prompting or manipulation. Here, the State failed to demonstrate that the circumstances surrounding the victim's statements support the reliability of those statements.

A police officer who lies to a suspect may, however, find the results of the interview accepted as "following from a reasonable interrogation technique." In *State v. Hatcher*, No. 99AP-460 (Mar. 17, 2000), the Ohio Court of Appeals was faced with an officer who explained his interview technique this way:

> Well, if you have certain facts that you believe that a suspect has committed, say they've done one thing, if you make it seem like the accuser is making it more, then it is easier for that person to say, oh, no, I didn't do that, but all I did was this. It's just a technique that we're trained to do.

The court concluded:

> Thus, regardless of this court's view of the use of lies by detectives as an interview technique during the course of questioning a defendant, we cannot find this factor alone supports a finding that appellant's confession was involuntary.

However, in a subsequent dissent, the court's decision was criticized:

> We simply should not sanction this "technique." The jury which heard the case was rightly concerned about the police conduct in this case . . . This technique is within the purview of our deliberation as an appellate court. Indeed, most courts, including many cited by the majority, have consistently disapproved of this technique as producing untrustworthy statements. Significantly, this court unequivocally did so in *State v. Johnston* (1990), 64 Ohio App.3d 238, which case the majority references, but fails to apply. We should clearly and consistently express ourselves about this technique and refuse to reward its use. Since the majority of this panel does not take that step, I respectfully dissent.

Two Missouri cases establish the proposition that Missouri courts have recognized that child witnesses are susceptible to suggestive interview techniques: *State v. Sloan*, 912 S.W.2d 592, 596 (Mo. App. E.D. 1995) and *State v. Foust*, 920 S.W.2d 949, 955 (Mo. App. E.D. 1996). Interestingly enough, neither *Sloan* nor *Foust* indicated that the complained of suggestive interview techniques or questioning affected the child witnesses' competency to testify. Rather, in both cases, the courts found that the trial court had erred by excluding testimony or questioning regarding suggestive interview techniques and whether the child witnesses may have been subjected to such techniques or questioning. In *Sloan*, the trial court erred by preventing the defendant from questioning a child witness about how her stepmother questioned her about the alleged abuse because such questioning did not constitute hearsay. It was not being offered for the truth of the matter but rather to establish how the witness perceived what her stepmother said and whether that affected her allegations of abuse.

PIAGET AND IMPLANTED MEMORY

In psychotherapeutic settings, when hypnotized subjects are regressed to a "past life" and are given suggestions that they were abused in their past life, many subsequently "remember" the suggested abuse and regard it thereafter as a fact. This phenomenon is not limited to the context of hypnosis.

One of the best-known examples of a false memory is found in the autobiography of developmental psychologist Jean Piaget (1896–1980). Dr. Piaget wrote that a kidnapping had been attempted on him when he was only two years old. He remembered copious details about the incident. Years later, however, the nurse who had reported the kidnapping attempt admitted that she made the entire story up to avoid being fired and to gain the good graces, even the gratitude, of the Piaget family.

As a child, Dr. Piaget had heard the story repeated so many times that he could not differentiate between his own memories and the false, imparted narratives that overtook his recollection. He would describe, with utter conviction, the assailants, the clothes he was wearing, how he was pulled by the kidnappers from his carriage, and the pain he experienced. He recalled all these details as if they were "real" memories. And being the memories of an educated and rational man—a professional psychologist, in fact—they remained unquestionably "true." But they were proven to be entirely false.

Children's cognitive abilities do not merely increase quantitatively. They go through stages that are recognized as being qualitatively different from one to the next. Childhood cognition and memory is fundamentally distinct from adult thought and recall. Most research confirms that the development of accurate recall skills occurs between the ages of 5 and 10. While younger children can be said to have memories, their linguistic inability to articulate them to others causes such "images" to disappear soon after formation. When a parent or other adult later relates their version of the presumably shared "memory," the child literally incorporates the story into his or her own inchoate version of it.

Another example of compromised memory is the victim who misidentifies a suspect due to an unduly orchestrated police lineup.

The fact that humans are prone to having memories implanted in this way has resulted in leading questions being ruled inadmissible in courtroom proceedings. Prospective jurors are often grilled as to their existing knowledge (usually gleaned from the mass media) of the case to be tried. During trials, jurors are sequestered, cut off from news sources, and not allowed to discuss the case outside the courtroom. Such steps are taken because we now know that the ability in adults to accurately remember events can be tainted to the point that their testimony is deemed "too unreliable to be admitted without offense to due process."

Some jurisdictions, including New Jersey, have even allowed trial courts to conduct "taint hearings" in cases where the defendant can produce some evidence that a child-victim's accusations are the product of suggestive or coercive interview techniques. Under New Jersey law, once the defendant establishes sufficient evidence of unreliability, the burden shifts to the state to prove by clear and convincing evidence that the child's statements are reliable.

Relying on a New Jersey Supreme Court decision, an appellant argued that a taint hearing is a valid pretrial procedure to investigate and determine witness competency and potential distortion of a child witness's memory. In *State v. Michaels* (1994) 136 N.J. 299, 642 A.2d 1372, a nursery school teacher was convicted of sexually abusing multiple children in her care. Significantly, extensive evidence presented in the case showed that the children were subjected to extensive, repeated, leading, and potentially hostile interviews and interrogations. In light of this evidence, the court was concerned that the use of "highly suggestive interrogation techniques" could have distorted the children's recollection of the events. As a result, the court held that a taint hearing was required under the state's evidence rules to determine "whether the pretrial events, the investigatory interviews and interrogations, were so suggestive that they give rise to a substantial likelihood of irreparably mistaken or false recollection of material facts bearing on defendant's guilt" [*People v. Montoya,* 149 Cal App 4th 1139, 57 Cal Rptr 3d 770 (Cal. App. 2007)].

FALSE MEMORY SYNDROME

In John Milton's *Paradise Lost,* Satan takes on the appearance of an angel and convinces an archangel entrusted with guarding creation to guide him to the Garden of Eden. There, Satan further deceives Adam and Eve and causes the fall of humanity. Milton used this biblical example of deceit to illuminate the human condition.

The professional, no matter how experienced, should resist the temptation to believe he or she is a human lie detector. False memories are all too easy to implant, and in their vivid imagery and wealth of detail, they can be indistinguishable from true recollections. Indeed, these memories are experienced as entirely real by those who possess them, and even after their unreliability has been exposed, they function to mask (or have perhaps entirely replaced) any original or true memory. The professional recognizes that any method of lie detection, including his or her own techniques, requires complete corroboration. Sincerity is what makes the self-deceived deceiver so convincing.

The name for this phenomenon is false memory syndrome: the belief that it is possible for one to remember in great detail events—especially traumatic ones—that did not actually occur.

Some people believe that the memory is like a computer hard drive that records every event accurately and keeps it intact. Research on memory has debunked that myth and has raised many questions about remembering and forgetting. Memories are malleable. They change incrementally each time we recall past events. With the passage of time, with direction or motivation, with the introduction of "interfering" facts, memory is inexorably transformed. When conducting an interview, the professional must be careful not to provide the subject with a trigger that will unconsciously transform his or her memory of an event to fit the interviewer's needs.

Recovered memory theory is now on the intellectual defensive. In 1992, a group of families torn asunder by false accusations of child abuse formed the False Memory Syndrome Foundation to combat the idea. Commentators have noted that the pendulum is now swinging the other way. Many psychotherapists now see recovered memory theory as a "'widespread and . . . damaging' fad." Michigan's common law recognizes a duty of care to third parties who might foreseeably be harmed by the mental health professional's use of techniques that cause the professional's patient to have false memories of sexual abuse [*Roberts v. Salmi*, 308 Mich. App. 605, 866 N.W.2d 460 (Mich. App. 2014)].

Much remains to be learned about human memory, especially about how both traumatic and nontraumatic memories are preserved. It has been shown that some of our memories can become "unavailable" to us. Furthermore, when such memories are seemingly rediscovered or uncovered, they can often be shown to be contaminated mixtures of both accurate and inaccurate information. Because of the reconstructive nature of memory, some memories may be distorted through influences such as the incorporation of new information, a factor that the professional must always take into consideration.

MEMORIES CREATED BY THE INTERVIEWER

The problem of tainted memory is much more evident in young children. The risk with young children is that they may be unable to distinguish between a memory of something that actually happened and a memory of something they only imagined happening. If an interview technique leads a child to imagine an event, the child's "memory" of that imagined event (the implanted memory) will be just as real to the child as memories of events he or she actually experienced.

In Arizona, *Doe v. Roe*, 191 Ariz. 313, 325, 955 P.2d 951, 963 (1998) and *Cecala v. Newman*, 532 F.Supp.2d 1118 (D. Ariz. 2007), the courts noted that repressed memories of childhood abuse can exist and that they can be triggered and recovered. They also concluded that other, equally real-seeming memories can be inaccurate, may be implanted, and may be attributable to poorly trained therapists or use of improper therapeutic techniques. Moreover, they concluded that juries must decide on a case-by-case basis whether either repressed memory recovery or false memory syndrome is at play.

Some investigators use the same technique to obtain information that conforms to their own prejudices. For example, in the following interview an experienced social worker, denoted "I," is interviewing a child, denoted "C." Occasionally, a police detective denoted "P" joins the interview.

The interview illustrates a number of inadvisable practices that are frequently seen in interviews by poor interviewers who are more interested in proving their theory about an incident than in working to uncover the truth about it. It serves as a model of what not to do to uncover the truth.

> ***I:*** We have gotten a lot of other kids to help us since I last saw you.
>
> ***C:*** No. I don't have to.
>
> ***I:*** Oh, come on. Did we tell you she is in jail?
>
> ***C:*** Yes. My mother already told me.
>
> ***I:*** Well, we can get out of here real quick if you just tell me what you told me last time.
>
> ***C:*** I forgot.
>
> ***I:*** No you didn't; I know you didn't.
>
> ***C:*** I did, I did.
>
> ***I:*** No, come on.
>
> ***C:*** I forgot.
>
> ***I:*** I thought we were friends last time.
>
> ***C:*** I'm not your friend any more.
>
> ***I:*** How come?
>
> ***C:*** Because I hate you.
>
> ***I:*** Is it because we are talking about stuff you don't want to talk about? What are you, a monster no? Huh? . . .
>
> ***C:*** I hate you.
>
> ***I:*** No you don't . . . You just don't like talking about this, but you don't hate me.
>
> ***C:*** Yes, I do hate you.
>
> ***I:*** We can finish this real fast if you just show me real fast what you showed me last time.
>
> ***C:*** No.
>
> ***I:*** I will let you play my tape recorder. . . . Come on, do you want to help us out? Do you want to help us keep her in jail, huh? . . . Tell me what happened to [three other children]. Tell me what happened to them. Come on . . . I need your help again, buddy. Come on.

C: No.

I: You told us everything once before. Do you want to undress my dolly?

❖ ❖ ❖

(Throughout, three asterisks indicate text omitted from the transcript of the testimony.)

P: She could never get out.

C: I know that.

P: Cause I got her. . . . She is very afraid of me. She is so scared of me.

I: She cries when she sees him [indicating the police detective] because she is so scared, . . . What happened to [another child] with the wooden spoon? If you don't remember in words, maybe you can show me.

❖ ❖ ❖

C: I forgot what happened, too.

I: You remember. You told your mommy about everything, about the music room, and the nap room. And all the stuff. You want to help her stay in jail, don't you? So she doesn't bother you any more. . . . Your mommy told me that you had a picture of yourself in your room and there was blood on your penis. Who hurt you?

C: [Child names the defendant.]

I: So, your penis was bleeding, oh. Your penis was bleeding. Tell me something else: was your hiney bleeding too?

C: No.

I: Did [the defendant] bleed, too?

C: No.

I: Are you sure she didn't bleed?

C: Yes . . . I saw her penis, too.

I: Show me on the [anatomical] doll . . . you saw that? Oh?

C: She doodied on me . . . She peed on us.

I: And did you have to pee on her at all?

C: Yeah.

I: You did? And who peed on her, you and who else?

C: [Child names a male friend.]

I: Didn't his penis bleed?

C: Yes.

I: It did? What made it bleed? What was she doing?

C: She was bleeding.

I: She was bleeding in her penis? Did you have to put your penis in her penis? Yes or no?

C: Yeah. . . . And I peed in her penis.

I: What was that like? What did it feel like?

C: Like a shot.

I: Did [friend] have to put his penis in her penis, too?

C: Yes, at the same time.

I: At the same time? How did you do that?

C: We chopped our penises off.

I: So, she was bleeding in her penis and you had your penis and your friend's inside her penis.

C: At the same time.[1]

This type of exchange is common in transcripts of child interviews and other subjects most vulnerable to suggestion. When, in this case, the subject says something that is not part of the interviewer's hypothesis (in this case, that the children chopped off their penises), the interviewer ignores it. There is no attempt to pursue it, probably out of fear that to do so might cause the child to further embellish the claim.

In this case, as in many others of its kind, the interviewer suggested the answers he needed to prove his initial hypothesis. He blatantly ignored responses that described acts that were physically impossible, and he never attempted to get at any truth that was not already a foregone conclusion.

---

[1] Excerpted from Stephen J. Ceci, "False Beliefs: Some Developmental and Clinical Considerations" in Daniel L. Schacter (Ed.), *Memory Distortion: How Minds, Brains, and Societies Reconstruct the Past* (Cambridge, MA: Harvard University Press, 1995).

CONFABULATION

Some people, though not actually cunning, intentional liars, are simply unable to tell the truth. The condition known as confabulation is a memory disturbance characterized by verbal statements inaccurately representing memory, background, or present situations. Confabulation is considered "honest lying" and is distinct from deliberate lying because there is typically no intent to deceive; such individuals are unaware that their information is false. Those who confabulate are generally very confident about their recollections, despite evidence contradicting their truthfulness.

"Confabulation is a process by which the witness fills gaps in memory with false and imaginary information . . . and comes to believe in the truth of his reconstruction" [*People v. Alcala* (1984), 36 Cal.3d 604, 620]. The best-known causes of confabulation are traumatic and acquired brain damage (e.g., aneurysm, edema), and psychiatric or psychological disorders (e.g., schizophrenia, bipolar disorder, or dementia). The professional interviewer must hone his or her ability to recognize a confabulator—a person who, clinically speaking, cannot tell the truth—because the confabulator, judging by tests and all other indications, appears to be a truthful person. Usually, confabulation does not benefit subjects. They are motivated by nothing other than the desire to relate their thoughts and experiences.

Confabulations, though not true, are not lies. They are the product of a psychological problem that the interviewer must understand before drawing any conclusions about the degree of truthfulness in the subject's responses.

The United States Supreme Court has observed a means by which the potential for confabulation may be avoided. It found that the basis for the excited utterance exception to the hearsay rule is that such statements are given under circumstances that eliminate the possibility of fabrication, coaching, or confabulation, and that therefore the circumstances surrounding the making of the statement provide sufficient assurance that the statement is trustworthy and that cross-examination would be superfluous [*Idaho v. Wright*, 497 U.S. 805, 820, 110 S.Ct. 3139, 111 L.Ed.2d 638 (1990)]. Therefore, a statement relating to a startling event or condition that occurred while the declarant was under the stress of excitement caused by the event or condition may be admitted into evidence under the excited utterance exception to the rule against hearsay [*Robbins v. State*, 300 Ga. 387, 389 (2), 793 S.E.2d 62 (2016); *Jenkins v. State*, 812 S.E.2d 238 (Ga. 2018)].

Regardless, problems of confabulation and suggestion are magnified by certain investigative techniques that the professional should avoid. Often the person interviewed will develop a rapport with the interviewer and subconsciously wish to please by giving answers that the subject believes the professional desires. This risk is particularly high when the subject has a substantial interest in the outcome of the investigation. These answers then become part of the subject's memory. The more a witness repeats his or her story, the more fixed it becomes in his or her mind. In addition, by asking questions in a certain manner, the interviewer may unintentionally supply information that gets incorporated into the subject's memory.

Confabulation is what happens when the brain tries to fill in missing pieces of data. It is part of a natural reflex that is similar to what happens when there are gaps in our physical vision. There is an actual hole in your visual field, the "blind spot," where the nerve sensors receive no light. But even if you close one eye and look, you are not aware of it. The brain fills in the missing information. That is what also happens when there is a memory lacuna: the brain literally tries to bring in extraneous information to fill in this big, empty space.

Because of problems with this hypercompliance in the confabulator, a subject will refuse to admit to memory imperfections or gaps. The subject will instead attempt to fill in those gaps. This could produce a recall of an event comprising all the following elements:

- relevant actual facts.
- irrelevant actual facts taken from an unrelated prior experience of the subject.
- fantasized materials (confabulations) unconsciously invented to fill gaps in the story.
- conscious lies—all formulated in the most realistic fashion possible.

Dr. Martin T. Orne, one of the foremost experts on the subject of hypnosis, has observed that the concept of hypersuggestibility is related to the phenomenon of confabulation. He points out that the same process that increases suggestibility by permitting the subject to accept counterfactual suggestions as real also makes it possible for the subject to accept approximations of memory as accurate.

The risk of confabulation is especially great during posthypnotic suggestion when the hypnotist suggests that the subject will clearly remember the forgotten event when the subject has no actual memory of the event. The subject may feel pressured to respond to the hypnotic suggestion as a result of a desire to please the hypnotist. In addition, the subject tends to respond literally to hypnotic suggestion. These factors enhance the potential for the hypnotized person to "remember" events that actually did not occur.

An excerpt from an interview with a person whose statements qualify as confabulations follows:

Q. Can you tell me a little bit about yourself? How old are you?

A. I'm 40 . . . 42. Pardon me: 62.

Q. Are you married or single?

A. Married.

Q. How long have you been married?

A. About four months.

Q. What's your wife's name?

A. Martha.

Q. How many children do you have?

A. Four. [He laughs.] Not bad for four months!

Q. How old are your children?

A. The eldest is 32, his name is Bob, and the youngest is 22, his name is Joe.

[These answers are close to the actual age of the boys.]

Q. [He laughs again.] How did you get these children in four months?

A. They're adopted.

Q. Who adopted them?

A. Martha and I.

Q. Immediately after you got married you wanted to adopt these older children?

A. Before we were married we adopted one of them, two of them. The eldest girl Brenda and Bob . . . and Joe and Dina since we were married.

Q. Does it sound a little strange to you, what you are saying?

A. I think it is a little strange.

❖ ❖ ❖

Q. Do you really believe that you have been married for four months?

A. Yes. . . .[2]

Psychological research supports the conclusion—one that is so important to professional interviewers—that remembering is a constantly reconstructive process and that distortions occur and accumulate at every retelling.

MEMORY DISTORTION

The memory traces of events we have experienced are stored randomly. Human memory is like a fragmented computer hard drive, with bits and pieces of a file in various places. The difference is that, with a computer's hard drive, you can run defragmenting software to correctly rearrange the bits and pieces. There is no defragmentation software for the human brain.

In a system that does not honor time or order, the possibility of one memory event influencing another is very great, especially if they bear some similarity to each other. Similarly, if the assignment of remembered events to their proper context and sequence depends on strategic retrieval, then post-event suggestions, which themselves become randomly stored memory traces, can later be mistaken for (and in effect take the place of) the "true" or original memories.

The professional knows from experience that even normal, healthy people confabulate all the time. We all add certain nuanced elaborations or distortions each time we relate a story (usually to make it reflect better on us), but these ego-based creative *re-rememberings* are sufficiently small that they have no real effect on the general truth of

---

[2] Excerpted from Ceci, "False Beliefs."

the complete story. They can be cleared up with further detailed questioning and investigation.

Although the interviewer wishes that the ability of human beings to remember were perfect, the best to be expected is that on most occasions human memory is sufficiently reliable. When precision of content and sequence is demanded, however, as it is in eyewitness testimony, human memory is notoriously poor and frequently distorted. The professional recognizes the irony that eyewitness testimony that is not corroborated is the least reliable of all forms of evidence.

Human beings are not computers. Memory is not hard-wired. It is almost never recovered in exactly the same way as it was recorded. Memory is a process that can be distorted and manipulated by events, by new information, or by a talented but unscrupulous interviewer.

14

False Beliefs

As we've seen in preceding chapters, false statements can be the result of the subject's conscious, deliberate decisions or the unintended output that results from certain cerebral conditions. The professional must recognize the difference between the two during the course of the interview. Deliberate lies may be intended to flatter, avoid punishment, gain rewards, or protect loved ones, while a false belief or confabulation may arise from a chain of inferences or reconstructive memory processes operating at a level far below the subject's own awareness.

Research into false beliefs abounds. To name one example, psychologist Stephen J. Ceci has written about cases that every professional can learn from. They make clear that memory is flexible and that the expression of the truth concerning events is always colored by subjective experience as well as, notably, the individual's innate need to believe that he or she is a good person, or, at least, not a bad person. One of Ceci's examples follows.

JACK HAMILTON: ASSUAGING A GUILTY CONSCIENCE

Ceci recounts the case of a pitcher who, on one particular occasion, threw an infamously destructive fastball and managed to persuade himself it had been entirely accidental.

In the 1960s, Tony Conigliaro was a slugging sensation with the Boston Red Sox and the youngest major leaguer to have hit 100 home runs. In 1967, Conigliaro's career was jeopardized when he was hit in the head with a fastball by pitcher Jack Hamilton of the California Angels. Suffering a fractured cheekbone, a dislocated jaw, and seriously blurred vision, Conigliaro struggled on for two more seasons before his injuries forced him to retire. On the occasion of his death in 1990, *New York Times* sports writer Dave Anderson interviewed Jack Hamilton, the pitcher whose fastball had nearly killed his opponent. As you would expect, Hamilton expressed sincere regret over the incident but asserted, as he had maintained for years, that he had not been trying to hit Conigliaro:

> It was like the sixth inning when it happened. I think the score was 2 to 1, and he was the eighth hitter in their batting order. . . . I had no reason to throw at him.
>
> I tried to go see him in the hospital late that afternoon or early that evening but they were just letting his family in.

Both of these "recollections" were contrary to fact. The first comment was a memory reconstruction that provided Hamilton with a logical framework that allowed him to maintain his belief that he did not deliberately throw at Conigliaro's head. In fact, the pitch that hurt Conigliaro happened in the fourth inning at a point when there were two outs and no one was on base. The situation called for a brush-back pitch. Conigliaro was batting sixth in the order, and he had amassed 20 homers and 67 RBIs that season, so he represented a real threat at that point in the game.

The second recollection is a similar reconstruction of memory, apparently intended to assuage Hamilton's conscience. He stated that he tried to visit the hospital immediately after the game, but in fact he did not go until the following afternoon. We know this because it was a night game. Hamilton selectively, if unconsciously, reconstructed his recollection and gave an account that permitted him to view his role in the termination of Conigliaro's career (and nearly his life) as being completely accidental.

The professional interviewer understands that people remember what they want or need to remember. Between the occurrence of an event and the interview about that event, the subject has sufficient time and opportunity to construct a memory that is easier on the conscience. The statements the subject later produces are false, but, as in Mr. Hamilton's case, the conviction that they are true is real.

FREUD: THE CRYPT OF MEMORY

Even Sigmund Freud, the famous psychiatrist, was subject to false beliefs. Freud learned that he had inadvertently taken credit for an idea one of his colleagues had shared with him several years earlier. He wrote to a colleague excitedly to tell him about his new theory of original bisexuality and was crestfallen to be reminded that the colleague himself had actually first articulated the theory during an evening walk they had taken together in Breslau years earlier.

This phenomenon of suppressing memories that do not serve our purposes or do not reflect well on ourselves is now discreetly referred to as "cryptomnesia." It occurs when a forgotten memory returns without it being recognized as a memory. The person believes it is something new and original. It is a memory bias whereby a person may falsely recall generating a thought, an idea, a song, or a joke. The person is not lying and is not deliberately engaging in plagiarism, but rather is experiencing a memory as if it were a new inspiration.

Thus, that most professional of professional interviewers, the father of modern psychoanalysis, found that he had created a false memory. He learned, and taught, that the interviewer must assume that any person can create a false memory without the least intention of lying.

MY FATHER: THE INSULT THAT NEVER WAS

My father, rest his soul, thought he was a great poker player. He was not.

He would play poker every week with his brother-in-law, my mother's brother. It was a friendly pastime with little cash involved since neither could afford to lose money in a mere game.

At a certain point, the weekly games came to an abrupt end. According to my father, sometime during that last game my uncle had called him a poor poker player. This was not actually what had happened. What really happened was that my father had lost $5 in the game and just could not abide taking on such a large loss. As a result, he concocted the false memory of a stinging insult and claimed to be so offended that he refused to speak with my uncle for 15 years. His false, self-implanted memory of the insult to his poker prowess resulted in a family dispute, a disruption that lasted until shortly before my uncle died.

We often detect quite easily the disjuncture with reality in the words of those suffering under the delusion of a false belief. In fact, the Texas courts [*Rich v. Rich,* 615 S.W.2d 795, 797 (Tex. Civ. App.—Houston [1st Dist.] 1980; *In re Estate of Harrell* (Tex. App. 2018)] defined the term *insane delusion* as "the belief of a state of supposed facts that do not exist, and which no rational person would believe." There has been little, if any, reason to enlarge upon that definition, but neither has there been any real effort to prescribe a detailed and reliable test of sanity.

If a person under an insane delusion as to existing facts commits an offense in consequence thereof, is he or she thereby excused? The answer must depend on the nature of the delusion. For example, if, under the influence of his delusion, a person supposes another man to be in the act of attempting to take away his life and he kills that man, as he supposes, in self-defense, he would be exempt from punishment [*Diestel v. Hines,* 506 F.3d 1249 (10th Cir. 2007)].

Each of these examples reveals an aspect of false belief, the inability to distinguish between real and imagined sources of input into the memory system. The California Angels pitcher, Sigmund Freud, and my father all invested in the reconstruction of personal memory and created false memories. Through selective memory and nuanced language, they set up the conditions whereby their erroneous version of reality became their "true" memory, in the service of psychoemotional needs. Jack Hamilton, the Angels pitcher, needed to believe he hit Conigliaro accidentally; Freud did not want to believe he was so unprofessional as to be capable of stealing another's ideas; and my father could not live with the knowledge that he had squandered the princely sum of $5 on a poker game.

SUGGESTIBILITY AND CHILDREN

In outlining his seduction theory, Freud claimed that many reports of childhood sexual abuse by female adult patients were likely false and that they only reflected the inability of children to distinguish reality from fantasy. This theory has never been considered a persuasive one, nor has it ever received widespread support, because, as most psychologists point out, in prior eras the reality of intrafamilial sexual abuse was simply not accepted. For the interviewer, however, Freud's claim raises certain points with regard to the power of suggestibility.

Children of different ages, when asked to state whether a particular word had actually been spoken in an incident or had only been imagined, respond differently. Six-year-olds have more difficulty discriminating between these two possible sources of their "true" memories than do children nine years of age or older.

The ability to differentiate between self-generated fantasies and memories of incidences of actual behavior (so-called realization judgments) is not developed before late childhood. Psychological source monitoring studies suggest that children can be susceptible to a wide range of misattributions, some of which involve confusing actual events with suggested events, especially when these events are perceptually and semantically similar.

Children can easily be confused by what others tell them or by leading questions. Studies reveal that psychologists' procedures in therapy or in repeated interviews can taint a young child's understanding of the past. For example, valid recollection may be tainted by the suggestibility of such techniques as "memory work," imagery inductions, or fantasy play. To the extent that such techniques can actually overwrite part of a child's memory, the interviewer should be wary of using them.

These and other psychological studies should lead the professional to conclude that eyewitness testimony is unreliable and that eyewitness statements from children are the most unreliable. The professional corroborates statements by:

- documentary evidence.
- physical evidence.
- videotapes of the incident.
- photographs.
- the testimony of other eyewitnesses.

Furthermore, the interviewer who believes children cannot lie is also committing self-deception. As every parent knows, children's statements can often be a combination of some parts truth, some parts linguistic ambiguity, and a great deal of innocent but "creative" elaboration. Without probing, checking, and corroborating a child's statements, no parent can determine the degree of truth in them.

To summarize:

- Memory retrieval is never perfect.
- Children are highly susceptible to suggestibility.
- Suggestibility can come from both external and internal sources.
- Children can easily misinterpret what adults say and vice versa.
- Passionate or emotional statements are not necessarily true.

INNOCENT DECEPTION AND LIES

Lies and deceptions come in many shades and are ubiquitous in normal daily life. Some forms of deception are even necessary to maintain decorum; white lies, skillfully delivered, allow for smoother social functioning. Most people who employ such innocent deceptions have no intention of harming anyone. They are, by and large, ordinary citizens merely trying to get services or money they think they need.

How, then, does the objective interviewer interpret deceptive behaviors, contradictory information, and highly suspect statements? When do mistakes, misdirections, and so-called misspeakings become lies?

In *Patients Who Deceive: Assessment and Management of Risk in Providing Health Care and Financial Benefits,* Lorne Pankratz wrote:

> I consider distortions to be those colorings of truth that result from observing the world through the tinted glasses that all of us wear. Deceptions, on the other hand, are the pictures carefully painted to lure others into seeing a new reality. These pictures provide a background, create a mood, capture attention, and display a story. The assessment process requires an evaluation of what information each picture distorts, manufactures or withholds.
>
> The distortions that arise from ordinary tintings must be understood to avoid labeling them as abnormal and deceptive. . . . social factors, the patient's emotional state, belief factors, and unintentional errors complicate matters for both the patient and the clinician.[1]

Distortions are not lies by the above definition, but they are as dangerous to an investigation as deliberate lies. The professional interviewer recognizes the propensity of most people to engage in unconscious deception. True professionals never accept a subject's statements as pure gospel; instead, they systematically narrow down the possibilities to find the objective truth and work to corroborate the statements with documentary or physical evidence.

---

[1] Pankratz, L. (1998). *American series in behavioral science and law. Patients who deceive: Assessment and management of risk in providing health care and financial benefits.* Charles C Thomas Publisher.

DELUSIONS

A delusion is defined as a persistent belief that, despite having no demonstrable basis in fact, the delusion will never be changed by use of reason. Similarly, a hallucination is a perception with no corresponding objective reality. Thus, in either instance, the person is not negligently interpreting actual facts but instead is out of touch with reality.

A person with a fixed false belief (a delusion) cannot testify in court. Before the court can reject the testimony, it must establish the following conditions, as must the prudent interviewer:

- The witness suffered from schizophrenia, paranoid subtype, a chronic mental illness evident in her medical records for some years.
- The witness's psychiatric history, despite intervals of lucidity, indicated that he was never free from the effects of the illness from its onset.
- A significant feature of the illness was a fixed false belief.
- The delusion was medically diagnosed as typical of schizophrenia paranoid subtype or other product of the brain disease, incapacitating recall.
- One characteristic was the inability to make a decision.
- The illness made the witness highly susceptible to the influence of others (delusions and influence-susceptibility are linked).

The prudent interviewer must be able to determine whether the subject is untruthful or is simply deluded, hallucinating, or out of touch with reality.

15

The Insurance Examination under Oath

The "examination under oath" is a formal type of interview authorized by an insurance contract. It is taken under the authority provided by a condition of the insurance policy that compels the insured to appear and give sworn testimony on the demand of the insurer. A notary and a certified shorthand reporter are always present to administer the oath to the person interviewed and record the entire conversation.

The lawyer (in simple cases, an adjuster or investigator) is retained to represent the insurer and questions the person interviewed in a manner similar to a deposition in a legal proceeding. Because of the formality of the proceeding—it includes an oath and the presence of the certified shorthand reporter—the task of establishing rapport with, and obtaining information from, the person interviewed is more difficult than in a standard interview.

The examination under oath, a tool for gleaning the maximum amount of information, is an effective weapon against insurance fraud. Often, however, the purpose of the examination under oath is not to stop fraud but rather to allow insured parties the opportunity to prove their claim of loss in cases where evidence has been destroyed by a casualty or is otherwise unavailable.

Almost every first-party property insurance policy contains a fraud and concealment provision that will generally void the policy where an insured attempts to defraud the insurer [*Leasure v. MSI Ins. Co.*, 65 Cal.

App. 4th 244, 248, 75 Cal. Rptr.2d 900 (1998)]. An attempt to defraud or deceive the insurer may take place in order to obtain benefits. To void the policy, however, the insured's misrepresentation must relate to a material matter [*Claflin v. Commonwealth Ins. of Boston, Mass.*, 110 U.S. 81, 94–95, 3 S. Ct. 507, 28 L.Ed. 76 (1884); *Cummings v. Fire Ins. Exch.*, 202 Cal.App.3d 1407 1416, 249 Cal. Rptr. 568 (1988)]. Moreover, to void the policy, an untrue statement must be knowingly and intentionally made, with the intent to deceive or defraud the insurer [*Pedrotti v. Am. Nat'l Fire Ins. Co. of Columbus, Ohio*, 90 Cal. App. 668, 671, 266 P. 376 (1928)]. See also *Claflin*, 110 U.S. at 95, 3 S. Ct. 507; *Cummings*, 202 Cal. App.3d at 1416–17, 249 Cal. Rptr. 568. Thus, where a plaintiff knowingly and willfully, with intent to deceive the insurer, makes false statements as to material matters in the course of the insurer's investigation of his or her claim, the defendant is entitled to summary judgment on the plaintiff's breach of contract claim.

Whether a false statement was in fact made is generally a question of fact to be decided by the jury. However, where a plaintiff admits to making false statements with the intent that his or her insurer rely on those statements, the issue of whether such false statements were made need not be tried [*Ram v. Infinity Select Ins.*, 807 F. Supp. 2d 843 (N.D. Cal. 2011)].

TAKING AN EXAMINATION UNDER OATH

The examination under oath is usually conducted by an attorney for the insurer, but the law does not require the presence of an attorney; any person appointed by the insurer can take the examination. Similarly, the insured is permitted counsel, if desired, but the presence of counsel is not a legal requirement. If the insured opts for it, his or her attorney has no right to ask questions or offer information during the examination.

Regardless, the wise interviewer allows the insured's attorney to ask any question he or she wishes and to elaborate on any facts, since this will further the purpose of the examination—to get as much information as possible. The professional prefers to learn what the insured has to say immediately rather than during later litigation.

In cases where more than one insured is named on a policy, the insurer may, depending on the state or the policy language, compel the insured(s) to testify separately outside the hearing of the other insured(s). Subjects will provide less guarded responses if they know that a coinsured is being questioned as well. Separate examinations under oath, exactly like separate civil interviews, lead to more accurate information and less chicanery.

The Insurance Services Office appears to have modified its form of Homeowners' Policy–3 to avoid the impact of court decisions by specifically stating that the insurer can require each insured to appear and, furthermore, to testify separately, thereby avoiding the possibility of collusion.

The insured's counsel may object to the form of the questions posed. If the objection is well taken, it should be honored since the insured's goal is to get usable testimony. If the objection is not well taken, though, it should be ignored.

If the insured's attorney instructs the insured not to answer a material question, this can in itself be sufficient grounds to deny the claim. It constitutes failure to comply with the policy condition concerning examinations under oath. When faced with an instruction not to answer, it is often effective for the interviewer to say the following to the insured and his or her attorney:

> I respect your decision not to answer the question. I must advise you, however, that the insurance company I represent considers the question you have refused to answer to be relevant and material to its investigation. The company can, if you continue in your refusal, decide to deny your claim on that ground alone. I make no such decisions, so I will honor your decision not to answer and go on to other questions. I feel, nevertheless, that it is my duty to advise you of the rights you gave to the company when you acquired the policy. You can certainly reconsider your decision. Would you like to meet privately with your attorney to discuss this matter?

Usually, the insured and attorney then reconsider the potentially heavy consequences and answer the question.

There is no reciprocal provision allowing the insured to take testimony of representatives of the insurer. Attorneys for insureds will attempt to pose questions to the claims person. These attempts must be rebuffed politely and with good grace.

THE ROLE OF THE INSURER'S ATTORNEY

A well-executed examination under oath is not only one of the insurer's most effective weapons against insurance fraud, it can also be highly instructive for the lawyer. If an attorney is responsible for performing the examination, the lawyer must make clear that it is his or her obligation to provide sufficient factual information supported by legal authority for the insurer to make a decision on the claim. The adjuster or claims representative should also, if possible, attend the examination to help the attorney and to study questioning techniques. Attorneys, whose job it is to ask questions, will usually do a more thorough job of examination under oath than will insurance claims staff.

After the examination, the attorney can also give the adjuster or investigator legal advice as to the insurer's rights, duties, and obligations and the need for further investigation to corroborate some of the statements made during the examination.

Counsel's report should include all the facts necessary to support any decision, whether learned in the course of the investigation or from testimony at the examination under oath. The lawyer must analyze the facts in relation to statutory and case law; only then will counsel be in a position to make a fully informed decision on the claim.

More often than not, the examination will cause the insurer's attorney to recommend payment of full indemnity to the insured.

If the attorney advises the insurer that indemnity should *not* be paid, the claims person should carefully analyze the recommendations to independently verify that there are sufficient facts, supported by policy language and legal precedent, to support the conclusion. It is the claims person who makes the decision, not the attorney. Decisions made by insurers must sometimes be based on reasons other than the law.

Insurers should use the examination under oath tool judiciously. It should only be used in cases where the insured is unable to prove his or her loss, when the insured's proof is inconsistent or incomplete, or when the insurer has a reasonable belief that a fraud is being attempted. Used properly by insurers, lawyers, and insureds who are intent on providing (or obtaining) only the indemnity promised by a policy of insurance to which they are entitled, the examination under oath will help the insured and the insurer fulfill the promises they made each other at the inception of the policy.

16

A Summary of the Practice of Interviewing

DEVELOP THE ART

At the start of this book, I said that interviewing by professionals is an art that incorporates and uses scientific methods. As is true with any art, one does not become adept at interviewing by reading about the interview process. An interviewer, like an artist or a musician, must practice, practice, and practice still more.

The famous Cubist painters Picasso and Braque started out painting in the standard representational mode. In shifting to a progressive style of multiple and angular forms, these painters were able to capture not just the external features but the very soul of the subjects they depicted. Like an artist constantly striving for a truer rendition, the interviewer develops and applies new techniques to uncover the truth. The more you hone your expertise, the more you'll be able to obtain information without the person interviewed knowing he or she was interviewed.

PRACTICE

No matter how long the interviewer has been developing the art of interviewing, every interview that is conducted is "practice." No one in any walk of life ever becomes so proficient that he or she cannot improve. Attorneys, physicians, dentists, architects, and other professionals describe their efforts as "practices" not simply because they involve practical skills, but because they are constantly learning more and are developing professionalism. Interviewers who stop learning and attempt to rely on conducting interviews by rote will eventually find that their effectiveness seriously declines.

Professionals make a habit of determining which approaches and techniques have produced the truth in the past and of using those approaches as often as possible. They also analyze any weaknesses in past interviews so as to avoid such pitfalls in future. If an associate listens to the interview, the professional will ask for a critique. If audio or video of the interview is recorded, the true professional will play it back and study the entire interview with an objective and self-critical ear.

There is nothing "routine" about any interview. In fact, the process is guaranteed to be different every time. The effective interviewer has a flexible and creative personality, and each interview performed is a work of art more refined and expressive than the last.

THE SCIENTIFIC SIDE

Interviewing is concerned with observation, analysis, and classification of facts. The interviewer who comes into an interview with a preconceived conclusion has failed before the interview begins. The professional interviewer believes only what can be proven by objective, verifiable evidence.

Professionals do not limit their work to the interview. The preinterview background gathering, the organization of the facts collected in the interview, the correlation of those facts to physical evidence available, combined with the legal consequences of the statements—all these work to make up the scientific collation of facts that round out an interview.

DEMEANOR

An interviewer, no matter what the provocation, can never lose his or her temper. While it may be true that some interviewers force confessions with the presumed "technique" of shouting, threatening, and berating the subject, this approach seldom works. Such actions only serve to irritate the subject and destroy any latent inclination the subject may have to confide in the interviewer. In short, an interviewer who loses control of his or her temper loses control of the interview.

THE PROPER PERSPECTIVE

The interviewer should never appear to need the subject's detailed and factual account or to try too hard. The skilled interviewer, rather, creates the kind of environment wherein the subject realizes that telling the truth is both expected and to one's own benefit. Successful interviewing requires an air of steady confidence and cool detachment—a "soft-sell" versus a "hard-sell" approach.

FAITH AND PERSEVERANCE

Regardless of successes, every interviewer, at every level, hits dry spells. Professionals must maintain faith in the proven process, as well as in their ability to successfully conduct an interview. Masters of any profession, whether it be sport, art, or science, recognize that periods of depression and setback are inevitable, and that their response is to work hard to overcome such slumps. Master interviewers study technique, practice application of principles, review past mistakes, and perform interviews (of any kind) daily, confident that the truth is out there waiting to be found.

PREPARATION

An interview cannot work if the interviewer is unprepared. Before the interview begins, the interviewer must seek to know as much as possible about the person to be interviewed. If a profession or trade is involved, wise interviewers will make themselves conversant with the basic language and processes of the trade, business, or profession.

EVALUATION

As important as the interviewer's questioning techniques is the interviewer's ability to evaluate the information uncovered by the interview. To determine the truthfulness of any subject's statements, the interviewer interprets an accumulation of data ranging from physical clues and verbal responses to the findings of background research.

If the interviewer determines from all objective and subjective tests that the statements made by the person interviewed are true, the fact can be reported and the case can be closed. If, however, the statements are found to be false, he or she may need to seek legal advice as to the use of the information uncovered. With proper advice and counsel:

- a story may be published.
- a new business relationship may take shape.
- an insurance claim may be denied.
- an employee may be hired or fired.
- a police report may be filed advising the police that the person who retained the services of the interviewer is the victim of a crime.
- the results of the interview may be turned over to a prosecutor.
- the person interviewed may be prosecuted for criminal activities.

Never consider your interview complete until you have fully evaluated it, determined the truthfulness of the subject, and decided whether further investigation is required.

APPENDIX 1

Interview 1: Earthquake Loss

The testimony that follows concerns the 1994 Northridge earthquake and arose from a claim presented by a couple who were professional insurance brokers. By the time the following questions were asked, the insured had already testified that certain documents previously thought to be forgeries were actually true and accurate originals. When confronted with this new evidence, the witness insisted on claiming that the interviewer was mistaken.

This transcript presents an example of a gentle, low-key use of the "accusatory" approach, which was initially unsuccessful in the trial, but later proved to be a deadly blow to the position of the witness.

MR. ZALMA: This will be Exhibit 15. It's a document from The Sleep Shoppe. It bears invoice No. 01-8125, which just happens to be the same invoice number as what we showed you earlier as Exhibit 8. The same invoice number as Exhibit 8. Explain this to me. They're completely different in description and amount.

WITNESS: That's true. Yeah.

MR. ZALMA: And since Exhibit 8 was the only thing you ever bought from The Sleep Shoppe, how did this invoice come to be?

OPPOSING COUNSEL: I don't think she said she bought anything.

WITNESS: This is a canopy bed that I bought from The Sleep Shoppe.

MR. ZALMA: So, you did buy something from The Sleep Shoppe?

WITNESS: I guess I did.

MR. ZALMA: How come this purchase from The Sleep Shoppe on May 30, 1994, has the exact same invoice number as your estimate dated June 1, '94?

WITNESS: I have no clue.

MR. ZALMA: Isn't it true that you just erased everything in the description on that invoice and wrote in "Jessica's Brass Bed" in your own handwriting?

WITNESS: No.

MR. ZALMA: Have you any explanation how these two documents could come to be?

WITNESS: No.

❖ ❖ ❖

MR. ZALMA: Have you intentionally misrepresented any facts to me in this examination under oath?

WITNESS: No.

MR. ZALMA: Did you intentionally misrepresent any facts when you acquired the policy from [insurance company]?

WITNESS: No.

MR. ZALMA: Did you intentionally conceal [anything] from [insurance company]?

WITNESS: No.

MR. ZALMA: Have you intentionally concealed any facts from me during this examination under oath?

WITNESS: No.

MR. ZALMA: Did you inadvertently conceal any facts from me or my client when you presented your claim to [insurance company]?

WITNESS: [no response]

MR. ZALMA: Did you inadvertently conceal from [insurance company] any facts material to its underwriting decision when you acquired the policy from [insurance company]?

WITNESS: I think there were things . . . that were disclosed to [insurance company's agent] that were not disclosed to [insurance company] on the application, but I never saw the application prior to the time that you showed it to me.

MR. ZALMA: All right. And those were things like the fact that you were going to sue the builders or that you were having wall leaks?

WITNESS: Right.

MR. ZALMA: You disclosed them to [agent] but apparently he didn't disclose them to [insurance company].

WITNESS: That's correct.

MR. ZALMA: Did you hide from [insurance company] . . . fail to disclose, facts that you knew were important to the company's evaluation of your claim intentionally?

WITNESS: Repeat the question.

MR. ZALMA: Did you intentionally fail to disclose something to the insurance company that you knew would assist it in evaluating your claim?

WITNESS: No.

MR. ZALMA: Did you present a false claim to [insurance company] in any part?

WITNESS: No.

After the testimony was obtained, the transcript was forwarded to counsel. The insured read and, with the advice of her attorney, corrected the transcript to read as follows:

MR. ZALMA: This will be Exhibit 15. It's a document from The Sleep Shoppe. It bears invoice No. 01-8125, which just happens to be the same invoice number as what we showed you earlier as Exhibit 8. The same invoice number as Exhibit 8. Explain this to me. They're completely different in description and amount.

WITNESS: That's true. Yeah.

MR. ZALMA: And since Exhibit 8 was the only thing you ever bought from The Sleep Shoppe, how did this invoice come to be?

OPPOSING COUNSEL: I don't think she said she bought anything.

WITNESS: This is a canopy bed that I bought from The Sleep Shoppe.

MR. ZALMA: So, you did buy something from The Sleep Shoppe?

WITNESS: I guess I did.

MR. ZALMA: How come this purchase from The Sleep Shoppe on May 30, 1994, has the exact same invoice number as you estimate dated June 1, '94?

WITNESS: ~~I have no clue.~~ I fabricated the document.

MR. ZALMA: Isn't it true that you just erased everything in the description on that invoice and wrote in the "Jessica's Brass Bed" in your own handwriting?

WITNESS: ~~No.~~ Yes, I erased everything with 'white-out' and inserted a new description.

MR. ZALMA: Have you any explanation how these two documents could come to be?

WITNESS: ~~No~~. Yes, I fabricated the document.

❖ ❖ ❖

MR. ZALMA: Have you intentionally misrepresented any facts to me in this examination under oath?

WITNESS: ~~No~~. Yes.

MR. ZALMA: Did you intentionally misrepresent any facts when you acquired the policy from [insurance company]?

WITNESS: ~~No~~. Yes.

MR. ZALMA: Did you intentionally conceal from [insurance company]?

WITNESS: ~~No~~. Yes.

MR. ZALMA: Have you intentionally concealed any facts from me during this examination under oath?

WITNESS: ~~No~~. Yes.

MR. ZALMA: Did you inadvertently conceal any facts from me or my client when you presented your claim to [insurance company]?

OPPOSING COUNSEL: Let me object, simply because the word "conceal" is extremely vague and ambiguous in this context.

MR. ZALMA: Understood. Let me ask another question, and I'll come back to it. Did you inadvertently conceal from [insurance company] any facts material to its underwriting decision when you acquired the policy from [insurance company]?

WITNESS: I think there were things . . . that were disclosed to [insurance company's agent] that were not disclosed to [insurance company] on the application, but I never saw the application prior to the time that you showed it to me.

MR. ZALMA: All right. And those were things like the fact that you were going to sue the builders or that you were having wall leaks?

WITNESS: Right.

MR. ZALMA: You disclosed them to [insurance company's agent] but apparently he didn't disclose them to [insurance company].

WITNESS: That's correct.

MR. ZALMA: Did you hide from [insurance company] . . . fail to disclose, facts that you knew were important to the company's evaluation of your claim intentionally?

WITNESS: Repeat the question.

MR. ZALMA: Did you intentionally fail to disclose something to the insurance company that you knew would assist it in evaluating your claim?

WITNESS: ~~No~~. Yes.

MR. ZALMA: Did you present a false claim to [insurance company] in any part?

WITNESS: ~~No~~. Yes.

When asked why the insured's lawyer "allowed his client to correct the transcript of the examination under oath to admit to the crime of insurance fraud and to an intentional misrepresentation and concealment of material facts sufficient to allow the insurer to declare the policy void," counsel could only reply, "I did so to prevent a charge of perjury."

I include this example to illustrate that the interviewer should always ask the ultimate question. Invariably, the witness will deny lying or doing anything wrong. If they do, they face the very serious charge of perjury if, eventually, further or cumulative evidence proves they lied. If they tell the truth, as this witness did, they lose their claim and face, in many states, a charge of insurance fraud.

In the case cited above, my client, offended that an insurance professional would attempt to defraud, declared the policy void and filed suit in U.S. District Court for treble damages under the Racketeer Influenced and Corrupt Organizations Act (RICO). At the time of this writing, that suit is still progressing, and the Fraud Division of the California Department of Insurance has begun criminal investigation proceedings. The witness was convicted of insurance fraud and received a suspended sentence. Her husband claimed to be an innocent spouse and settled with the insurer.

APPENDIX 2

Interview 2: Cross-Examination of Expert on False Memory

The following transcript excerpts are from the cross-examination of a physician whose testimony concerning the testimony of a child was proved to be unsupportable in *State v. Molen*, 2010 -Ohio- 1908 (Ohio App. Dist.2 04/30/2010). The court of appeals noted that counsel obtained important concessions from the expert physician concerning children's ability to remember. The key points, as we saw earlier, are:

- that memory retrieval is never perfect;
- that children are more susceptible to suggestibility;
- that suggestibility can come from both external and internal sources;
- that someone can suggest something to a child that may not have occurred and that doing so may result in the child perceiving the event as having occurred and reporting that it did occur;
- that false disclosures by preschoolers may be the result of misinterpretation by the child or misinterpretation by the adult to whom the report is made; and
- that specifically in this case, Dr. Miceli has had experience with subjects being passionate about something they actually know not to be true.

"Dr. Miceli has never been called as an expert witness 'by anybody other than [the] state of Ohio.'" (Trial transcript at 567.)

"Dr. Miceli has never 'taught a seminar for any defense lawyer organizations.'" *Id.*

"Dr. Miceli's role is not that of an independent investigator; her role was that of Z.D.'s therapist; her job was to be 'supportive and helping.'" *Id.* at 568.

"Bedwetting can be normal for little boys up to five or six years old." *Id.* at 569.

"Dr. Miceli is not aware of the statistic regarding bedwetting that 'it is normal in 75% of boys after five and six but there's 25% where it's not normal for these kids.'" *Id.* at 569.

"It is not necessarily unusual that bedwetting occurs at ages of eight or nine after it had stopped at age three." *Id.* at 569–570.

"Bedwetting 'can keep going if there's still turmoil.'" *Id.* at 570.

"If a person is repressing memory, it does not mean that internal conflict has gone away." *Id.* at 570–571.

"In relying on reported 'history' and relying on what she has seen, Dr. Miceli has in the past 'of course' been wrong." *Id.* at 571.

"In 2004 and 2005, Dr. Miceli conducted seminars in which she made presentations to other psychologists on the subject of children who witness violence." *Id.* at 571–572.

"'Children who witness domestic violence display various emotional, physical and behavioral disturbances'; they experience feelings of anger, fear, guilt, confusion, helplessness, withdrawal, low self-esteem, nightmares, aggressive behavior against peers, family members, and property." *Id.* at 573–574.

"Kids who witness domestic violence suffer physical problems such as bedwetting, insomnia, diarrhea, and stomach problems." *Id.* at 574.

"Children who witness domestic violence have difficulty concentrating." *Id.* at 575.

"Children who have witnessed domestic violence experience the same type of trauma or emotional disturbances as children who have been sexually abused." *Id.* at 575.

"If a child saw a parent being choked, spit on, or called vicious names, this would cause the child to experience some of the aforesaid types of trauma or emotional disturbances." *Id.* at 575.

"Six to ten year old boys typically are not as mature as girls of the same age." *Id.* at 577.

"'A lot of boys now are much more informed' about sex; it's a 'different world.'" *Id.* at 578.

"The American Psychological Association Journal of Social and Personal Psychology is a respected journal." *Id.* at 579.

"Dr. Miceli is aware of studies that [suggest] playing violent video games, such as Mortal Combat, is correlated to a person's aggressive thoughts, feelings, and behavior." *Id.* at 579.

"Dr. Miceli has heard of the 'mature rated games' of Mortal Kombat and Doom that contain gore, blood, and violence." *Id.* at 580.

"Dr. Miceli does not disagree with a study that indicates that 'children who are being predisposed to aggressive [sic] may become more aggressive with this exposure.'" *Id.* at 581.

"Defense Counsel presented to Dr. Miceli a study involving college students which established that even a brief exposure to violent video games can temporarily increase aggressive behavior." *Id.* at 581.

"It is possible that even brief exposure to violent games by a child can increase the child's aggressive behavior." *Id.* at 582.

"Memory is 'very constructive'; 'memory storage is both emotional and cognitive.'" *Id.* at 583.

"If there is 'a mismatch between what we expect and what we actually experience, it's not uncommon for us to resort back to what is expected to be in our memory.'" *Id.* at 583.

"There are three phases of memory: encoding, storage, and retrieval." *Id.* at 583–584.

"The final step in memory—retrieval—is 'never perfect.'" *Id.* at 585.

"Suggestibility can impact 'what we think that we're retrieving.'" *Id.*

"Children, especially preschool children, are more susceptible to unconscious suggestibility." *Id.* at 585–586.

"Someone can suggest something to a child that may not have occurred that results in the child perceiving it as having occurred and reporting that it did occur." *Id.* at 586.

"Someone can suggest something to a child that the child does not decipher as 'the real or fake,' but becomes part of memory." *Id.*

"When the child retrieves that 'fake' thing, 'it still comes out as if it was something that happened.'" *Id.*

"Suggestibility can come from both external and internal sources. If someone is afraid or emotionally aroused, it can distort what that person is perceiving or what that person believes he is perceiving." *Id.* at 587.

"'None of this [is] an exact science' and 'there are margins of error.'" *Id.*

"Dr. Miceli described both the normal and abnormal behavior of a preschooler sexually acting out." *Id.* at 588.

"Sexualized behavior could indicate inappropriate boundaries of the home such as children witnessing parents in sexual activity." *Id.* at 589.

"Children's appropriate behavior 'in terms of showering together, in terms of physical contact, etc.' can contribute to some sexual acting out." *Id.* at 590.

"Preschool children and elementary teachers see children sexual[ly] acting out." *Id.*

"Dr. Miceli explained false reports of sexual abuse. For instance, a child who reports that his bottom hurts—which may be the result of a father 'wiping when they had a bowel movement' or spanking—may result in the other parent jumping to the conclusion that the child was sexually abused and then reinforcing that false belief in the child." *Id.* at 592.

"Dr. Miceli introduced Z.D. to an eight-week group session involving two to three boys in which they 'talk about school, talk about behavior, talk about anger, talk about families. We talk about sexual abuse.'" *Id.* at 593.

"In the group session, the boys disclose their sexual abuse, the 'ramifications of what happened to them,' and how people did or did not pay attention to them after their disclosure." *Id.* at 594.

"Based upon the fact that Z.D. had made a disclosure, Dr. Miceli 'went with that'; she did not conduct a forensic interview; she did not conduct an objective hypothesis-testing interview." *Id.* at 595–596.

"A child having difficulty walking or sitting may be a physical symptom immediately after anal sexual abuse." *Id.* at 597.

"Dr. Miceli's job is to 'help children.'" *Id.* at 600.

"Observing domestic violence is a form of abuse." *Id.*

"Some children exhibit traumatic behaviors before disclosure and some after disclosure." *Id.* at 601.

"Some children do fight back, but most do not." *Id.* at 602.

"A child who pees on himself could have a problem and may not have a problem." *Id.*

"It is not unusual for a child to be told more than once to clean his room or brush his teeth." *Id.*

"It is not unusual for a child to forget to bring homework home on four or five occasions; it may be the result of laziness or a failure to write down the assignment." *Id.* at 603.

"It is not unusual for kids to get an attitude." *Id.* at 604.

"False disclosures by preschoolers may be the result of misinterpretation by the child or misinterpretation by the adult to whom the report is made." *Id.* at 604–605.

"There are 'other reasons, other motivations' for a preschooler to say something happened that didn't happen." *Id.* at 605.

"When asked, 'Do you always know when someone is lying to you?' Dr. Miceli replied, 'Of course not, nobody does.'" *Id.*

"'If a person is extremely emotional and passionate about a thing and they're telling you that thing,' that does not necessarily make it true." *Id.* at 606.

"Dr. Miceli has 'had experience in that situation with someone being passionate about something and it not being true.'" *Id.* at 606.

"Mr. VanNoy's recross-examination of Dr. Miceli covered the following items:"

"Post Traumatic Stress Disorder (PTSD) can occur over a period of time; there is not [a] test to determine the exact date and time when it occurred." *Id.* at 620.

"Witnessing a mother being kicked, hit, and spit on is a traumatic event which can cause a child to feel helpless and experience emotional turmoil." *Id.* at 621.

"Dr. Miceli has no personal knowledge as to whether Z.D. attempted to drown a dog or his baby brother." *Id.*

"It is possible that young people Dr. Miceli has dealt with have purposefully lied, but she 'didn't catch them lying.'" *Id.* at 621–622.

"If the perpetrator of the abuse is still living in the house, in half the cases the child will report the abuse, while in the other half the child will not report the abuse." *Id.* at 622.

"Mr. VanNoy questioned Dr. Miceli regarding a study 'that indicates that 74% of the disclosures by preschoolers are accidental.'" *Id.* at 623.

"Dr. Miceli testified that 'typically it is an accidental discovery.'" *Id.* at 624.

"Dr. Miceli has never treated individuals who have been falsely accused. However, she has 'had some families that I've worked with where there have been inaccurate reports, things that the children have said while they were in family mediation.'" *Id.*

(Trial court's March 16, 2009, Decision and Entry at 15–20).

APPENDIX 3

Interview 3: Elizabeth Loftus on False Memory Syndrome

Deception poses one of the greatest dangers to others when it is disguised by sincerity and when the self-deceived deceiver lies by telling what he takes to be the truth.

Some experts believe they can detect deception, whether it be self-deception or a blatant lie. Many professional interviewers believe that they can tell when a person they interview is being truthful. However, the professional should resist the temptation to believe he or she is a human lie detector. False memories are all too easy to create, and they sometimes bear many of the trappings of true recollections, including vivid imagery and specific detail. Indeed, these memories can become so real that those who claim them may find it difficult to remember the truth—to see anything but the false memory—even after their errors are exposed. The professional recognizes that any method of lie detection, including the professional's experience and skill, must be able to account for these very real false memories and should exercise caution before using any method of lie detection or determining whether a person interviewed is truthful. Physical evidence and other corroboration are needed.

What follows is an edited transcript (as recorded at *http://criminaldefense.homestead.com/Loftus.html#anchor_8,* which now requires a password) of the direct examination and cross-examination of Dr. Elizabeth "Beth" Loftus, professor at the University of California at Irvine and nationally known expert in the controversial fields of "unreliable eyewitness testimony," "suggestive interrogation," "false memory," and "recovered memory." I have deleted the commentary and reproduced only the testimony. Dr. Loftus is relied upon by many courts, including those referred to in Chapters 13 and 14 of the present volume.

The testimony is self-explanatory and does not need commentary. It makes clear that relying on eyewitness testimony is extremely hazardous and that an effective cross-examination can reduce the effectiveness of an expert who claims the testimony is unreliable. As you read the transcript, consider whether it gives you any hints about how to conduct a professional and detailed interview without suggesting answers or causing confabulation.

DIRECT EXAMINATION OF FALSE MEMORY EXPERT

By Dick Degeurin, counsel for the defendant

(Three asterisks indicate text omitted from the transcript of the testimony.)

❖ ❖ ❖

A: My name is Elizabeth Loftus.

Q: Is it Dr. Loftus?

A: That's fine, Dr. Loftus, yes.

Q: You're not a medical doctor; you're a Ph.D. in psychology; is that correct?

A: Correct.

❖ ❖ ❖

Q: I'd like for you to, if you will, tell the ladies and gentlemen of the jury a little bit about your qualifications. First, your education.

A: Well, I guess, beginning with college, I was an undergraduate at UCLA. I received a bachelor's degree in mathematics and also in the field of psychology. It was awarded in 1966, and I left UCLA. I moved to Stanford University. I received a master's degree in psychology in 1967, followed three years later by a Ph.D. of psychology in 1970. So, that's the major educational background.

Q: And it's the Ph.D. that allows or sometimes qualifies one to be called a doctor?

A: Correct.

Q: But not a medical doctor?

A: No, I'm not medical doctor.

Q: Have you made a study of memory during your professional lifetime?

A: Yes. Within the field of psychology, my major specialty is human memory, eyewitness testimony, and other topics related to the subject of memory.

Q: Let's talk a little bit first about your teaching experience. Have you taught in the field?

A: Yes, I have. Well, basically, after I got my Ph.D., I left Stanford. I spent three years teaching in graduate school in New York City. And then, in 1973, I joined the faculty of the University of Washington in Seattle, and I have been a regular faculty member at the University of Washington teaching there with occasional teaching at other institutions.

Q: What are some of those other institutions?

A: In 1975–76, during that academic year, I was at Harvard. I taught a course in law and psychology. In 1986, I was a visiting professor at the Georgetown University Law Center which is the law school associated with Georgetown University.

Q: That's Georgetown in Washington, D.C., not Georgetown, Texas, right?

A: Yeah.

Q: Did you know there was a Georgetown, Texas?

A: No, I didn't know there was a Georgetown, Texas. I'm sorry. In Washington, D.C., yes.

Q: Okay.

A: And the other teaching I've done, I believe it was 1975 to 1987, I taught in the summers at the National Judicial College which is a school for state level judges at the University of Nevada.

Q: Is that a school for people that want to be judges or people that already are judges?

A: People who already are judges. Some of them are newly appointed to the bench or newly elected and some are long-term judges.

Q: Let's talk just a minute about some of the honors and awards that you've received through the years. Hit the high points for us. What are some of the first honorary degrees you got, the honor societies, and so forth?

A: Well, I'm not sure how much detail you want. I have been awarded four honorary doctorates for my research, primarily in the area of memory. So, the first one was from Miami University in Ohio in 1982. I delivered the commencement address in conjunction with that award. I received an honorary doctorate from Leiden University which is a major university in The Netherlands. I received an honorary doctorate of law from John Jay College of Criminal Justice. That is part of the City University of New York's educational system. And the last one was from the University of Portsmouth, an honorary doctor of science awarded just a couple of years ago, and Portsmouth is in England.

Q: Have you been invited to teach and have you taught at various law enforcement academies and schools?

A: I have. In fact, just a few months ago, I was teaching FBI agents in the state of Washington. Periodically, over the last 30 years or so, I have been invited to speak to law enforcement, state patrols, and to various groups of judges in California, Michigan, and Kansas. Just a few examples of ones that come to mind.

Q: What is your primary area of study in lecture and teaching?

A: I teach courses in cognitive psychology which is the psychology of perception, memory, thinking, problem solving, all the higher mental processes. Then I teach more specialized courses in the area of human memory. I also happen to teach a regular course on eyewitness testimony. These are regular courses at the University of Washington, apart from the lecturing that I do on an occasional basis to different groups or organizations that want to learn something about this subject.

Q: In the field that you have dedicated your professional life to, are there both studies of experiments in memory and recall and actual empirical studies of what has happened in real cases? Tell us a little bit about those.

A: Okay. The way in which we gather information about eyewitness testimony, scientific information or information that is utilized by researchers, is twofold. First, there are experimental studies and I, in my laboratory at the University of Washington, in my research program, I do lots and lots of experiments to understand what kinds of things cause eyewitnesses to be accurate or what kinds of things cause them to make mistakes. What factors are important in leading a witness to be able to give accurate or, conversely, mistaken testimony. But we also utilize collections of wrongful convictions, particularly a collection compiled by the Department of Justice, the U.S. Department of Justice. These are cases of known wrongful convictions, and we try to analyze these cases to figure out what went wrong. Of course, in the vast majority of these cases you see some problem with eyewitness testimony as a major cause of wrongful conviction. So that's another source of data for our understanding of the mental process of eyewitnesses.

Q: The Department of Justice, of course, is the federal department that oversees all of the prosecutions in federal court throughout the country, is that correct?

A: That's correct. They happen to have issued an extensive report in 1996 called "Convicted by Juries, Exonerated by Science" which is a report about 28 cases of wrongful conviction, individuals who were later exonerated through DNA analysis.

Q: And that's—to shed a little light on it—that's a report by the actual prosecutorial branch of the federal government on prosecutions that have gone awry. They are actually saying: We found that these are bad prosecutions because of these reasons?

A: They were certainly mistaken prosecutions or mistaken outcomes.

Q: Have you made a career and a life study of this phenomenon of eyewitness identification and the things that affect and influence this reliability?

A: Yes, I have. I mean, I've spent the last 30 years doing experiments on the subject; but we think of this not just as eyewitness identification because the broader umbrella is memory. Eyewitness identification often refers to the ability to see a person and later to identify, you know, somebody that you may or may not have seen before. But many times witnesses are remembering other kinds of details, details about who did what or details about, you know, where someone was at what time or details about license plate numbers. And this falls within the general subject matter of eyewitness testimony. So, that's why I like to use the more general term "eyewitness testimony" to include eyewitness identifications.

Q: Of course, you know that one of the questions in this case is a license plate number?

A: I do, yes.

❖ ❖ ❖

Q: Have you . . . before we get into some specific questions about that . . . have you written what's generally considered to be the bible on eyewitness testimony?

A: Well, I wish someone would say that. I have written at least four books and scores and scores of articles in the area of eyewitness testimony; but there are also many other scientists, psychological scientists who have worked on this subject, who have written excellent books and many, many hundreds of articles.

Q: Defendant's Exhibit 11 is a 30-page document that contains a list of your writings, your teaching, the places where you've lectured and spoken and so forth, correct?

A: Yes.

Q: If I were to go down the list and ask you about each of these things, would this be an accurate reflection of what your answers would be?

A: Yes.

DEFENSE COUNSEL: We offer Defendant's Exhibit 11.

PROSECUTOR: May I see it, Judge?

DEFENSE COUNSEL: Sure. I'll give them a copy.

PROSECUTOR: No objection.

THE COURT: It is admitted.

DEFENSE COUNSEL: Of course, I'm not going to go through everything. I just want to give the jury an idea of what's here. We probably can't read this, but just to give the jury an idea, this Defendant's Exhibit 11 includes your personal data, education, teaching experience, honors and awards, and professional memberships?

A: Maybe you can focus it.

Q: I'm trying. That's a little better. I just have to move it up and down the screen. Professional memberships, other professional experience, government and other consulting, then books that you've written or co-authored and articles that you've written and professional journals, '68, '69, '70, '71, so forth. Police officers' journals.

Did you write for police officer publications also?

A: I have, yes.

Q: Journal of Police Science and Administration?

A: Yes.

Q: We get down to 1999, so far, and then places you've been invited to address is the next listing, correct?

A: Yes.

Q: Baylor, you've been to Baylor?

A: Yes.

Q: Twice in one year it looks like. Is that right?

A: Looks like it. You skipped over Rice and [the] University of Houston.

Q: I just thought it was remarkable that you've been to Baylor.

A: Oh.

Q: Okay. You've testified frequently, haven't you?

A: I have over the last . . . since 1975, maybe 230 times.

Q: Has your testimony always been in criminal cases or not?

A: No. I would say of those 230 cases, maybe a hundred or so might be criminal cases, and the others would be civil cases. It's just an estimate.

Q: So, approximately a third of the time that you've testified in court, it's been in criminal cases, and the other two-thirds would be, of course, in civil cases?

A: Right. Just a rough estimate. Maybe it's two-fifths of the time in criminal cases.

Q: Okay. Have you consulted with the prosecution in some cases?

A: Numerous times, yes.

Q: On the other hand, has most of your testimony when called in criminal cases been from the defense side of the case?

A: In all but one of the criminal cases, I've been called to testify by the defense. One. In one case, I did testify in a jury trial when called by the prosecution.

Q: Is there a reason for that? Is there a reason why it seems to be that you've been called most often by the defense in a criminal case, as opposed to by the prosecution?

A: Yes. I think there is probably a very good reason.

Q: What's that?

A: Well, there is scientific evidence that shows when eyewitnesses are testifying, sometimes it can be very persuasive testimony, even when it's wrong or even when it's got some serious problems. Usually my research focuses on what some of those problems with eyewitness testimony might be under certain conditions.

❖ ❖ ❖

Q: Now, you're not going to testify in this case and you don't testify in cases that somebody didn't see what they said they saw.

A: No. Without independent corroboration of some sort, you can't, no. Occasionally it's possible to find out that, you know, the human eye could not have possibly seen that detail at that distance. But for the most part, no, you can't say whether the witness was right or wrong, only that certain factors may be present that lead an average person to make a mistake.

Q: And you're not here to testify that someone's right or wrong, but only to offer your expertise on what might affect the accuracy of eyewitness testimony?

A: Absolutely. Yes.

❖ ❖ ❖

Q: Tell us generally, then, what are the things that we should look for. What are the things that affect the reliability of someone who says, "I saw something." What are the things that affect how the jury should judge that?

A: Well, the first thing you need to realize is that memory does not work like a videotape recorder. We don't record an event and play it back later. The process is much more complex, and I think. . . .

THE WITNESS: Your Honor, if I could illustrate this for the jury?

THE COURT: You may step down if counsel asks you to.

THE COURT: You need to keep your voice up when you're away from the microphone, please.

THE WITNESS: Okay, thank you.

DEFENSE COUNSEL: May I stand at the lectern, Judge?

THE COURT: Yes.

❖ ❖ ❖

A: To answer the question and set the important factors in the context of the process of eyewitness testimony, you need to realize that we divide the process into three major stages. So, first there is the acquisition stage. Here's a period of time where some event occurs and some information is laid down in a witness's memory system. Then the event is over, time is passing, and we refer to this second stage as the retention stage. And finally, you might approach a witness and ask certain questions or ask the witness to make an identification, ask the witness to retrieve information from memory. We call this the retrieval stage. Our job as researchers in this area then is to identify the factors that come into play in each of these three stages that affect the accuracy of someone's recollection. So, I can go into as much detail as you have time for.

❖ ❖ ❖

Q: I'm not going to go into a whole lot, but I want to ask you a couple of questions about that. The retrieval phase is when someone reports what they saw, right?

A: Yeah, there are factors that come into play at this stage of the process that affect the accuracy of what somebody is telling you.

Q: That's what I want to ask you about.

A: Okay.

❖ ❖ ❖

Q: What can affect the accuracy of that retrieval stage? That is, a typical situation where someone sees an event and then hours or days or weeks later is asked to report about that event.

A: I think I can best answer that by backing up just a little bit and starting with this retention phase. And I think it's something of a matter of common sense that the longer the passage of time, the less good your memory's going to be. But there's some other aspects that are not a matter of common sense.

So, the longer the retention interval, the worse the memory. If I were to plot how good memory is, as a function of time passing, whether it's seconds or minutes or days or weeks, you expect to see some sort of a forgetting curve that might look like this. It's something of a matter of common sense that memory fades over time.

What's not so much a matter of common sense is that as this memory is fading, it becomes more and more vulnerable to what we call post-event information. And by this, we mean new information that becomes available to a witness after the event is completely over. That new information can sometimes supplement a person's memory, alter the memory, distort the memory, and contaminate it.

So, one of the factors that affects the accuracy of retrieval is whether there has been post-event information that's perhaps misleading in some way.

Q: Would post-event information include, for instance, seeing a newspaper or television report that had the picture of a suspect in the case?

A: Oh, absolutely. Out in the real world, that is one of the key ways in which witnesses to some event get new information, especially if it's a high publicity event. They see photographs or they see witness descriptions or whatever in the media and it can act as post-event information and can supplement or alter somebody's recollection.

Q: If a person is shown, for instance, a lineup that is not put together very well so that the suspected person resembles the description of the culprit but none of the others in the lineup resemble the culprit, can that be the kind of post-event information that affects memory?

A: Well, we don't usually call that post-event information. I would ordinarily see that put under the category of a biased testing situation. So, if you give somebody a test, it might be a photographic array and the witness is asked to pick out the person they might have seen before; if there is one person in that photographic array who matched some prior description, then many witnesses will often fasten on that one individual whether that person is the right person or the wrong person. And, of course, once that selection is made, it then influences everything that happens after that.

❖ ❖ ❖

Q: Is there such a thing as encouraging or supporting a questionable identification once made?

A: Well, when you ask that question, you're asking about a very important factor that many experts have studied and testified about, and it's called the confidence factor. When somebody, say, makes an identification or makes a retrieval, tries to answer a question based on their memory, they often will express their level of confidence when they do that. And one of the things that the studies have shown is the relationship between how confident somebody is about their identification and how accurate they are is actually a very weak relationship.

A person on the street thinks it's a strong relationship, but the scientific work in the area shows it's a very weak relationship. That means it's common to have people who are very confident and wrong as well as other times people who are very confident and right.

The other important aspect of confidence is that confidence is malleable. So if you take a person who expresses a level of confidence who says, "I'm 80 percent sure," and you start giving them feedback and in some way communicating, even inadvertently, "You picked the right person, the one we think you should have picked," that confidence grows. They aren't more accurate, but their confidence gets stronger. That's what we mean by the malleability of confidence.

Q: So then with some support from others, some suggestion that the witness picked the right person, the confidence level grows?

A: Excuse me for interrupting. Dr. Gary Wells from Iowa State, one of the leading researchers in the eyewitness area, has studied the malleability of confidence. One of the ways in which he gets this confidence to be artificially inflated is by saying to the witness, "Good, you picked the suspect." I have actually heard him give a speech in New Orleans just a few weeks ago in which he talked about one case in which, after an identification was made, the people in the police station started clapping. I'm simply saying that giving an eyewitness positive feedback can artificially bolster the witness's confidence.

Q: Could facial expressions do the same thing?

A: Absolutely. Anything that conveys the idea that you picked the right person, you picked the person we hoped you'd pick, whether it is done verbally, with gestures or however.

Q: You talked about the retention period; the longer the retention period, the memory curve goes down. If the retention period is very short, that is, if the retrieval of the acquisition of the event follows soon after the acquisition of the event, then the chance for a memory fade to be at work here is less, right?

A: Yes. I mean, that's implied by this forgetting curve. If somebody is trying to retrieve information after a very short period of time, generally the memory is going to be at its strongest. There hasn't been time for it to decline. There hasn't been time for the witness to be exposed to post-event information.

Now, that doesn't necessarily mean that the person is always accurate because there can be some sort of perceptual error. You see something and in the short period of time it takes to look away and try to remember it, you're actually introducing some error.

❖ ❖ ❖

Q: Let's talk about that—the perception phase which I think is also the acquisition phase. Acquisition is when you get the information from the event, but perception is how you perceive it, correct? Explain that.

A: Well, we talk about perception being sort of the storage of information into the memory system, sort of what gets in in the first place. Kind of what gets in at the time of the event. What gets in in the first place may not necessarily be accurate. It might help if I introduce a concept here called the span of apprehension.

Q: Span of apprehension. Explain.

A: Yeah. If I ask you to look at something, depending on how many items you have to look at, you will be able to report some of them immediately. If you look at something briefly and then that object is taken away, and you have to report what you saw, if it's one or two items or four items, people can be fairly accurate in reporting back what they saw. As you start to increase the number of items, you start to introduce errors because we can only hold in mind so much information after a single glance.

Q: Is there a way in which the mind works in this kind of perception phase; that is, let's say you have a string of letters and numbers. If you're raised to read from left to right, instead of down the page as in China or across from right to left as in Arabic countries, if you're raised to read from left to right, are there studies that show in a string of numbers or letters where the most inaccuracy comes?

A: You know, I wish I had reviewed all of that information before coming here today; but I cannot name a study for you. There are . . . there's a hundred years of studies on the span of apprehension that show that, you know, basically if you've got three or four or five items, you make relatively few mistakes if you look at something and try to repeat it. But if you start adding items, the mental task gets a little bit more difficult and you are going to make mistakes. It's a normal process. I believe that, when we're talking about people who read from left to right, the items in the primary primacy position, the ones on the left are going to be a little more accurate than the ones in the middle or the ones on the right.

Q: So, does the science tell us that it's possible for someone to see a series of numbers and to then write down what that person perceives and still that person might be mistaken?

A: Oh, absolutely. I mean, you know, the more items you have to hold in mind, the more likely it is you're going to make a mistake on one or more of the elements. It would be very normal and customary for someone to see something and write it down slightly mistaken. Maybe it only happens 10, 15, 20 percent of the time, depending on how you test the person and depending on the size of the set that they have to hold in mind. But it's . . . it would be a normal perceptual error.

[The defense asks the expert to explain the principle of redundancy.]

Q: Okay. Is there a principle dealing with this in science called redundancy?

A: There is a principle called redundancy and to the extent that you do have redundancy, that can help you.

Q: Explain that. What does that mean?

A: For example, if we call up to get a telephone number, I mean, and we . . . it gets a little harder now that the area codes are changing all the time, but it used to be that we really wouldn't have to really rememorize the area code because it was always the same. So, you could get a set of numbers and repeat them back and add the area code because it's redundant. It's frequently used with the numbers in that area.

Q: Is that why usually when you call information, they'll give you the number twice?

A: Well, you know, a phone number contains seven items. Sometimes people do have trouble with seven items. We think we can hold maybe five items, sometimes six items much of the time, not all of the time; seven items much of the time, but not all the time without a mistake.

❖ ❖ ❖

Q: Well, back to the retrieval phase. In eyewitness testimony or in eyewitness situations, frequently the police will have some sort of identification procedure, either a photographic spread where a number of photographs are shown at the same time, sometimes a photographic spread is done with one picture being shown and taken back and then the next picture being shown and taken back and so forth in a series. As between these two methods, which is the best to avoid suggestiveness in trying to pick out the most similar person in a set of six?

A: Believe it or not, I understand that question. So if, for example, somebody were going to display to a witness a six-person photo spread, you could either display it simultaneously, laying out all six pictures as you see in this diagram . . . I hope you can see . . . or you could display Photograph No. 1 and take it away and then Photo No. 2 and take it away. One method is called the simultaneous method when all photographs are shown together as in this diagram and in the other is shown the sequential method. It's called the sequential method. The scientific work supports the benefit of showing things one at a time rather than laying them all at once.

Q: Why?

A: The reason is what witnesses often do when they look at a simultaneous array such as this, they'll figure out the person who best fits their remembered description. So, they are making what is called a relative judgment which is the person, relatively speaking, saying that person is the "closest" rather than what we would like them to do which is: Is that the person or not? That is one of the reasons why researchers have recommended this sequential approach, rather than the simultaneous approach.

Q: Would it make a difference in this comparison that it's human nature when seeing six photographs to compare and pick out the one that seems most likely, would it make a difference if the person trying to pick out somebody knew that there was a suspect in custody and that the suspect's picture was likely in that group.?

A: It does make a difference.

Q: Are there studies that show this?

❖ ❖ ❖

A: Yes. For many years people have done research and made recommendations and these recommendations are now actually incorporated into some guidelines put out by the United States Department of Justice that say: when you ask a witness to look at a photo spread or a lineup, it is important to give some sort of instruction that suggests that the person may or may not be in the photo spread or lineup. This is to make the witness feel comfortable in picking no one, if the witness wants to. If the witness doesn't know the suspect is in the photo spread or lineup, the witness won't feel forced to pick someone. So that kind of instruction is the recommended procedure.

Q: Would it make a difference if the witness had been informed, perhaps, not by the police that were showing them the identification procedure, but through rumor, through media reports or whatever source that the police did have a suspect in custody?

A: Well, I think it would increase the likelihood that the person would want to pick someone because witnesses do want to be helpful; they want to be cooperative; and they like to help solve crimes. It might increase the likelihood that they would choose someone.

Q: Okay. Now, let's talk about lineups. By that I mean live lineups or as we have in this case, videotaped lineups. What is the principle that should be followed where a suspect is in the lineup? Should you try to find fill-ins or "distracters," I think is the terminology? Should you try to find fill-ins that fit the description of the suspect, or should you try to find fill-ins that fit the description of the culprit?

A: Okay. Well, that is a difficult question to answer because in a typical case, the description of someone is somewhat consistent with the suspect. So, your goal is to try to create a test, whether it's a photographic test or whether it's a live lineup in which people fit the description of the perpetrator.

Now, when you have a description that is very discrepant from the suspect, then it's a little more difficult to figure out what to do. I mean, you may need at some point to have some people who match the suspect and some who match the description of the perpetrator. But the job is a little harder for law enforcement that have to construct these tests.

❖ ❖ ❖

Q: What about the showing of . . . I've been using the term "sequential" in other questions, but the showing of two different procedures, first, a photographic spread and then a videotape lineup, not having the person there live to see the people walk across the stage, but videotaping that, perhaps being affected somewhat by the quality of the videotape and then showing the videotape to the same person that's seen a photo spread with this key factor: That the only person in common in both procedures is the suspect?

A: That is a problematic procedure for the following reason: First of all, it has a name. It's called photo biased identification, and I'll just summarize it by photo biased identification and explain why I refer to this as problematic. We've talked about an event occurring and that someone later tries to retrieve information or make an identification, and I think we can all appreciate that in an actual case there are many acts of retrieval. So, when I draw one retrieval phase, I'm simplifying things tremendously. We've got many acts of retrieval.

If this retrieval is a videotape of a lineup that has been preceded by another act of retrieval which is a photo, we'll call it a photo lineup or a photo spread, then the act of looking at this photo spread, and especially when you select someone, can bias what happens afterwards. That's what a photo biased identification is. The work on photo biased identification was first published by Dr. Kenneth Diefenbacher [phonetic] who was a professor at the University of Nebraska. He demonstrated that by showing photographs in between an event and a lineup identification, you can dramatically increase the chances of a false identification.

To show you what I mean by "dramatically," in his particular research the chance of a false identification of an individual that the person had never been seen before was 8 percent. But if the individual's photograph had been seen during this interval of time before the lineup, then the chance of a false identification rose to 20 percent. So, you can see what is happening here. The person is looking familiar because their photograph was seen, not because they were seen in person at the time of the initial criminal event. And that's the phenomenon of photo biased identification. That's why it is somewhat problematic to have a situation that you described where the individual is in the set of photos and then there's another test and only one person from the first photo test stays in the second test.

❖ ❖ ❖

A: I'm going to mark, before we get out of control here, thus far these two diagrams that you've made. The first one will be No. 12, I believe, and the second, No. 13. Let me ask you a couple of other questions.

Q: Here's a hypothetical question. If a person perceives an event and within a few days goes through a lineup procedure, picks somebody out, says, "I wouldn't say for sure, but on a scale of one to ten, ten being the strongest identification and one being the weakest, I'm about 7. Suppose that person later sees a video lineup that has the same suspect that he's pointed out in the first lineup but no other persons from the first lineup and now says "I'm about 8 on the scale of certainty." And then suppose that about a year later that same person in court says, "Well, I'm about 9 on the certainty scale." Given that there is no other influence on the perception of the event, is what I just described an example of the evolving level of certainty?

A: You have just described a situation that resembles what I've tried to diagram here where you have an event and multiple acts of retrieval and one of the reasons why a person's confidence grows over these multiple acts of retrieval is because, indeed, when they keep on seeing the same person, that person does become more familiar and that can artificially enhance the certainty level. It's also possible that during this period of time, after the initial retrieval at 70 percent and before the later retrieval at the higher percent of certainty, that some new information became available. Suppose, he was told, "You know, you picked the person we wanted you to pick," or situation. That sort of exposure can artificially enhance the confidence level of a witness.

❖ ❖ ❖

Q: Let me give you another hypothetical situation. If a person perceives an event and, within a couple of weeks, is shown a video lineup and in the video lineup says, "When I close my eyes, the individual in Position 5 frightens me, and I think that's the culprit." Suppose that individual is then asked, "From a level of one to ten, how certain are you?" and that person then says, "Eighty percent." Then that person about a year later sees news reports that have the individual she picked out photographed on the front page of the paper and news reports. Then that person appears in court and says, "Now I'm 100 percent certain that that's the man." What's at work here?

A: It would be a similar kind of phenomenon—somebody who is looking at the individual again on a subsequent occasion. Of course, that person does look more familiar and sometimes that familiarity results in a higher reported confidence level. Also, the new information from the media could serve to inflate the confidence in the same way that it has in many of the studies done by Professor Wells.

Q: Now let me add something to that same hypothetical situation. Assume that in addition to what I've told you already that the original description given by this person of her assailant is that he had pantyhose over his face and that person does not describe a cap or hat. When that person testifies in court a year and a half later, that person then says, "I never said that he had a pantyhose over his face. He did have a cap on his head." Further assume that the husband of that person cannot identify the attacker but says that when he saw the attacker, the attacker had a cap on his head. Now, what factors are at work there?

A: Well, first of all, in that scenario that you've just described, it does appear as if the possibility of the introduction of post-event information is playing a role or could be playing a role in this case. If there is no recollection of any kind of [a] hat but a recollection of panty hose and another witness mentions a hat, many times witnesses will pick up information from other witnesses, a kind of post-event information, and they supplement or alter their own recollection with the new information. They aren't intentionally lying. It's just the way the memory works. So she may have learned that fact later and come to believe that she actually saw it herself, and that would be kind of normal memory supplementation through post-event information.

Q: I want to pick up on something you said. The person wouldn't be lying, but the person actually believes what she or he is saying?

A: Oh, absolutely. In our studies of post-event information, when we inject post-event information into people's conscious awareness by asking them leading questions or by exposing them to media coverage or by allowing them to overhear another witness's version, they pick up the information, and they come to believe it's their own recollection, and they are not intentionally lying. This has become their memory.

Q: Are there studies and have you studied and are there writings and publications that deal with this factor that a very exciting or frightening event affects perception, acquisition and the accuracy of a witness's report of the event? Am I stating that correctly?

A: Yes. There are a number of studies.

Q: Explain that to us.

A: Are you asking about the impact of seeing something that's very upsetting?

Q: Frightening.

A: Frightening? Traumatic?

Q: Sure, traumatic.

A: Well, there are a number of studies in which witnesses have been exposed to extremely upsetting material, and one of the things that these studies show . . . for example, in one of my own studies, we showed people a film in which a little boy gets shot in the face at the end of a bank robbery. It's a very upsetting film. We find that when people see these kinds of very upsetting films, it can, contrary to conventional belief that somehow some indelible fixation is created in the mind, in fact, it can lead to impairments in memory of the details of the event. In that particular research, people had more trouble remembering a variety of details when they'd seen this very upsetting and violent ending.

❖ ❖ ❖

Q: Doctor, just as we took our break, we started to talk about the effect of fright, excitement, [and] trauma on perception. I think it's safe to say that the general public's outlook on that is that if it's a frightening event you remember it better. Do the studies and the research reveal whether that is true or not?

A: Well, when somebody experiences something frightening, I mean, they often remember what type of event it was, for example, that it was an auto accident or a robbery and not something else. And they certainly often can remember some core details, but what many of the scientific studies show is that often some of the peripheral details, even the face of the person holding a weapon in a robbery, can suffer when there is extreme arousal and extreme fright.

❖ ❖ ❖

Q: Now, I want to talk to you about a principle called unconscious transference. First of all, what is that?

A: The definition of unconscious transference is it's a mistaken recollection where you confuse someone you've seen in one situation with someone you've seen in a different situation. The definition makes it a little hard to grasp, but the classic example that has been discussed whenever people are talking about unconscious transference, I think, helps us appreciate and understand what is meant by the term. And that example originally produced by Patrick Wahl in his book *Eyewitness Identification in Criminal Cases*, some 30 or more years ago, is an example of a train clerk who's held up in the train station. He goes to a lineup and identifies somebody in the lineup as the robber. And it turns out that the person who was identified was not the guilty person, not the robber, but someone who had purchased tickets from the train clerk on several prior occasions.

So, you can see what is happening in the situation. The clerk goes to the lineup and looks over the faces of the people. One of those people does indeed look familiar, and that familiarity is mistakenly related back to the robbery, rather than back to the purchasing of the tickets where it properly belongs. That's an unconscious transference, and that's the classic example of it.

Q: When he looks at the lineup, does the witness realize that the person he's identifying is not the robber but someone he's seen before?

A: No. Thus, the term "unconscious." The person is seeing someone who looks familiar. The familiarity is erroneously connected to the crime, rather than to where it properly belongs, and the witness is usually not aware of it at all.

Q: So, the witness can be sincere, can believe what he or she is saying but can be mistaken because of the phenomenon of transferring somebody he's seen someplace before subconsciously into somebody that's in the lineup?

A: Correct.

Q: Now, first, you've written tons and tons of stuff about this. Is what you've said today, can that be found in your writings? Is all of that in your body of work for the past 20 some odd years?

A: Oh, absolutely. I think my first book on eyewitness testimony was published in 1979 and reprinted more recently. But these basic ideas are things I've been writing about for 25 years and, of course, new studies are being done and new information is being acquired by the psychological researchers who study in this area. But, in essence, these are findings that have been around for a long time.

Q: As far as you and I are concerned, we met for the first time yesterday?

A: Yes.

Q: We talked on the phone, of course?

A: A few times, I believe.

Q: You've never appeared in a case in which I have appeared?

A: No, I don't think so. Not that I know of. I don't remember ever meeting you; but I don't know whether you might have worked on a case that I was working on as a separate attorney. Not that I know of. I am being cautious.

Q: And, of course, you expect to receive compensation for your research that I've asked you to do and your time in appearing here?

A: I hope so, yes.

Q: You will.

A: Okay.

Q: Your compensation is not based upon whether we win or lose, is it?

A: No, absolutely not.

Q: And, in fact, no one could pay you to change what's in your books?

A: I don't think anybody could because I've already said it in most of these books and articles. So, I'm really speaking it again. If I tried to say something different, somebody would probably notice.

Q: We know that you've taught FBI agents and secret service agents and other police agencies and written in police journals and so forth; but even though that's happened, are you very popular with prosecutors?

A: I have to say that the prosecutors don't seem too happy with me or with this kind of information or with people who . . . I mean, maybe just not me, but other researchers who work on these same issues.

Q: Is [sic] the research and the conclusions you've drawn from it and your writings and papers the mainstream of your body of work in this area?

A: Yes.

Q: And there are others, many others that agree with your work? Professionals, I mean.

A: Absolutely, yes.

Q: One final thing. You and I are going to appear to teach next month on a program coincidentally in Tucson, correct?

A: Well, yes. I was invited to lecture. It's the National Organization of Criminal Defense lawyers meeting, and I was actually surprised to see your name on that list, too.

Q: In fact, you're the one that told me we were both on the same two- or three-day program, right?

A: Yes.

Q: We offer Defendant's Exhibits 12 and 13, the charts that the doctor testified about.

PROSECUTOR: No objection.

THE COURT: They're admitted.

DEFENSE COUNSEL: No further questions at this time. We pass the witness to the prosecution for cross-examination.

❖ ❖ ❖

CROSS-EXAMINATION

By prosecutor

❖ ❖ ❖

Q: Good afternoon, Dr. Loftus.

A: Good afternoon.

Q: We've never met before?

A: Only just a few minutes ago.

❖ ❖ ❖

Q: Okay. And my name is [prosecutor's name], by the way. Can we have this understanding: I promise you that I won't be repetitious and waste your time if you can promise me that you won't try to help me by answering questions that I haven't asked, and you'll just answer my questions. Can we do that?

A: Yes.

❖ ❖ ❖

Q: Okay. First of all, it's true, isn't it, that you're testifying today in the middle of the state's case because my co-counsel [co-counsel's name] and I agreed to let that happen?

A: Well, I don't know the details of that, but I think that that's true.

Q: Because your understanding is we could have said, "No, we're not going to let her come to [the name of the city]. It's not time for the defense's case." And you wouldn't have been able to testify because of the conflicts in your schedule?

A: I think that's true, yes, unless some videotaping arrangements were made.

Q: Which we don't typically do in criminal cases in Texas. So, I guess you could agree with me, then, that [co-counsel's name] and I agreed to let you come in out of order so the jury could hear everything that you have to say. Do you agree with that?

DEFENSE COUNSEL: I think that calls for a conclusion behind them doing that, and I don't think it is proper.

THE COURT: That's sustained.

❖ ❖ ❖

Q: [By the prosecutor] Did I object one time during your testimony?

A: No, not that I heard. No.

❖ ❖ ❖

Q: And leaving prosecutors and how they feel about you aside for today, can we just agree that we'll talk about how others in your field feel about you?

A: That's fine.

Q: It's true, Dr. Loftus, that for many years, when you began your study in this field, many judges and many courts didn't let you testify before a jury?

A: That would happen occasionally prior to 1983, yes.

Q: Like I said, you don't need to help me because my question was: "In the beginning, when you testified, many judges and many courts didn't let you testify before a jury, did they?"

A: A number didn't, yes.

Q: Okay. And even today, in some jurisdictions in our country and in some courts, even in the State of Texas, your testimony doesn't always get to be before a jury?

A: I don't know the details of Texas, but it is true in other states occasionally.

Q: Are you familiar—'cause I know from reading your books and we'll get into that later, but I know that you—it seems like you pride yourself in keeping up with cases that happen around the country dealing with eyewitness testimony.

A: I try to, but there's so many of them that I can't claim to know about all of the cases.

Q: Do you know anything about the Weathered, W-e-a-t-h-e-r-r-e-d, versus State of Texas case? The opinion was delivered last week. Are you familiar with that one?

A: March 29th, it was. I believe.

Q: In that case, our highest criminal court held that the judge was okay in that case by not letting the jury even hear that eyewitness expert's testimony. Isn't that true?

A: That was the ultimate holding of the Court of Criminal Appeals.

Q: And like I said, Dr. Loftus, you don't need to try to help me. I'm going to ask my questions. A lot of times they are "yes" or "no" answers.

DEFENSE COUNSEL: Object to the side-bar remark.

THE COURT: That's sustained.

PROSECUTOR: The ultimate holding in this case delivered in March, this month, this year, our higher court said this judge was okay in not letting the jury hear anything that witness—that expert had to say?

A: I believe that's true. That was not me. It was a different expert.

Q: Yes ma'am. That's because a lot of people say—and let's leave prosecutors out of it. A lot of your people, psychologists, psychiatrists say it's just a kind of common-sense thing that Liz comes in and testifies about, right? Yes or no?

A: Well, no one would call me Liz because it's either Elizabeth or Beth.

Q: I'm sorry.

A: But I don't know if . . . I think it's misleading to say a "lot of people."

Q: Reputable people in your field say that, though, don't they?

A: A few quite reputable people have expressed that opinion. A few.

Q: Basically what you testify about is, it's not really hard science, it's more soft science and maybe even, if you want to be real blunt, psychobabble, right?

A: I don't think people in my field would call it that, no, even the very reputable people.

❖ ❖ ❖

Q: You don't? Okay. In your vitae here that y'all provided us with here today, I see a list of some articles and books that you've written. One of them is called "People Care in Fire Emergencies—Psychological Aspects"; "Calling Nurse Blaze: Tailoring Programs to Fit Human Behavior"; "How Deep Is the Meaning of Life"; "Insurance Advertising and Jury Awards"; "Hear Ye, Hear Ye"; "To File, Perchance to Cheat"; "Ten Years in the Life of an Expert Witness"; "How to Play to the Jury You Select in Complex and Other Cases"; "Money, Sex, and Death: Gender Bias in Wrongful Death Damage Awards"; "The Psychological Pay-Dirt of Space Alien Abduction Memories"; "Womb with a View"; "Memory Beliefs and Memory-Work Experiences"; "The Private Practice of Misleading Deflection"; "Who Is the Cat that Curiosity Killed?", all of these having to do with all sorts of things having to do with memory and perception?

A: Well, some of those have to do with perception or human information processing, yes.

❖ ❖ ❖

Q: Is there anything at all about memory or perception that you don't make money off of?

A: There's plenty that I don't make money off of, like freeing innocent people from prison when I do it pro bono, without any fee for my work.

PROSECUTOR: Judge, if I could just ask the witness to answer the question.

DEFENSE COUNSEL: I think that's responsive.

THE COURT: That's overruled.

Q: [By the prosecutor] I'm sorry. What was that answer again?

A: Some of my pro bono work is freeing the innocent.

Q: Are you here today pro bono?

A: No.

Q: What's the grand total amount that you expect to be paid when you get all done with this case?

A: I don't know yet, but it might be on the order of $10,000 possibly for all the work over the last few months.

Q: When did you come to Houston on this case?

A: Yesterday morning.

Q: What time did your plane . . .

A: I'm sorry. I left my home yesterday morning.

Q: What time did your plane hit the ground in Houston, Texas?

A: Well, it was delayed in a snowstorm. So, it was a little late. It was supposed to get in at 3:40.

Q: My question was: What time did your plane hit the ground in Houston, Texas?

A: I think it was possibly 4:15 maybe. It was late because of snow.

Q: Do you pay for your own plane ticket in town?

A: No. I had an e-ticket.

Q: Is that going to come out of your pocket or the defense's pocket?

A: It was paid for already. I picked up an electronic ticket when I got to the airport.

Q: Yes, ma'am. And who paid for that?

A: I'm not sure. I think the defense, I believe unless there was somebody else—I did not pay for it.

Q: Who pays for your hotel room?

A: I paid for my hotel room.

Q: They're not going to reimburse you?

A: Well, I hope they will; but I paid for it when I checked out this morning.

Q: Where did you stay last night?

A: At the Hyatt Hotel.

Q: Here in downtown?

A: Yes.

Q: And all of your meals while you're here in town, obviously, you're going to be reimbursed for?

A: Well, I only had one meal; but I hope to be reimbursed for it. It was $17.

Q: Okay. And all of the time you spent on the phone with the defense counsel, you get reimbursed for all those minutes you're on the phone?

A: I hope to be compensated for my time, yes. I hope to.

Q: Any research you did in this case at all, whatsoever, however important it was, you hope to be reimbursed for?

A: I hope so, yes.

Q: Because you don't work for free?

A: Unless I make that arrangement, which I do several times a year.

Q: But you didn't in this case?

A: But I did not in this case, no.

Q: What is your typical charge by the hour?

A: Well, it depends. If I'm doing it pro bono, it's nothing. If I make other arrangements, it's less. I sometimes charge $400 an hour for my time.

Q: Can we agree that for purposes of your testimony in this case, you ain't doing it pro bono. So, we can throw that out.

DEFENSE COUNSEL: That's repetitious, Judge.

THE COURT: That's overruled.

Q: [By the prosecutor] You're not here today pro bono, are you, Dr. Loftus?

A: Right. I think I said that already.

Q: So, what is your charge in this case?

A: I charge $400 an hour for my time.

Q: Does that include while you're on the airplane?

A: Well, generally I charge for up to a maximum of 12-hour days when I'm out of town. Even if I spend 16 hours that day, I would only charge for 12.

Q: So that could possibly include time spent going to the bathroom in the courthouse?

A: I hadn't looked at it that way.

Q: It could?

A: It could.

Q: When you add all that up, plane ticket, hotel, room, meals, plane ticket home, telephone calls, any research, going to the bathroom, fixing your hair this morning, sitting up there in that chair, the grand total that you're going to submit to defense counsel when you're all done with this is going to be how much?

A: Well, I've already said on the order of $10,000, maybe $11,000. I don't know what it's all going to add up to yet. Approximately.

Q: Have I left anything out that you typically charge for?

A: No, I don't think so.

❖ ❖ ❖

Q: During your direct examination with defense counsel, please correct me if I'm wrong, but I don't think I ever heard you mention the name [the name of the defendant]. Did that word ever come out of your mouth?

A: I don't think so.

Q: And during your direct examination by defense counsel, correct me if I'm wrong, but I don't think I ever heard you mention the name of [name of the eyewitness].

A: I don't think I mentioned the name, no.

Q: Do you know who he is?

A: Yes.

Q: Did you ever mention the name [name of the victim].

A: Not in my testimony.

Q: How about the name [name of another eyewitness].

A: No.

Q: How about the name [name of another eyewitness].

A: Those names didn't just slip your mind, did they?

A: No.

Q: Because, of course, you've spoken with all of them because that's why you're here today, to talk about their identifications. Have you spoken with them?

A: No.

Q: You've never talked with [name of the eyewitness]?

A: No, I haven't.

Q: You've never talked to [name of the eyewitness]?

A: No, I haven't.

Q: You've never talked to [name of the eyewitness]?

A: Correct.

Q: Have you ever talked to [name of the defendant]?

A: I may have said "Hello," but I don't know if I said anymore than that, and I'm not even sure that I said "Hello."

Q: When you got into town last night, you didn't have a conversation with him? You didn't speak to him? You didn't interview him?

A: That's correct.

❖ ❖ ❖

Q: When was it you were first contacted by anybody in regards to this case?

A: I think it was a few months ago. I don't remember exactly.

Q: Can you try a little harder? Which month?

A: I just don't remember. Maybe January.

Q: Who was it that first contacted you?

A: Either [name of defense counsel] or [name of defense co-counsel]. I just don't remember.

Q: Besides [name of defense counsel] and [name of defense co-counsel], have you ever spoken with anybody else in regards to this case?

A: Others from the office of [name of defense counsel].

Q: Like Ann?

A: Yes.

Q: Anybody else besides people in that office?

A: Other attorneys in the office.

Q: Nobody else outside the office?

A: Outside the office I may have mentioned to somebody who . . . a forensic psychologist who's a friend of mine in the Houston area . . .

Q: Would that be Dr. Edward Friedman?

A: No, I don't know that person.

Q: Have you ever spoken about this case with anybody in the defendant's family?

A: Well, I have met [given name of defendant] mother out in the hallway and had a brief conversation with her today.

Q: Other than that?

A: No.

❖ ❖ ❖

Q: Did you ever ask [name of defense counsel] if you could read or look at his notes from the police report?

A: I don't remember if I asked him that or not.

Q: Did you ever pick up the phone and call us and ask us if you could read the police report?

A: No, I didn't do that.

Q: Did you ever ask [name of defense counsel] if you could look at his notes from the witness's statements?

A: Well, I have read those. I reviewed all those. I didn't have to ask him. He sent them to me.

Q: He sent those to you?

A: Yes.

Q: Did you ever come down here and listen to the tape-recorded statements from [name of an eyewitness] and [name of another eyewitness]?

A: I read transcripts of their statements, their interviews.

Q: My question was: Did you ever come down here and listen to the tape-recorded interviews of [name of an eyewitness] and [name of another eyewitness]?

A: No.

Q: Because you know, based on everything you told us today, a lot of this is in the nuance, the voice inflection, the way the questions are phrased that you can't get just from reading the transcript. You need to hear it, based on what I heard you testify about earlier.

A: You can probably learn more from hearing something on top of actually reading it, yes.

Q: You could have come down here if you wanted to and asked to listen to the tapes yourself?

A: Well, I think that would have added a tremendous expense.

Q: It sure would.

A: Unnecessary expense.

Q: Unnecessary expense?

A: That's my opinion, that it would have added an unnecessary expense.

Q: You think it would be an unnecessary expense for you to be able to listen to the voices of the witnesses to the murder when you never even bothered to pick up the phone and call him [indicating the defense attorney]. That is to you an unnecessary expense?

A: It might have provided a little additional information, but it would have been . . .

Q: "Additional" to what? From what I heard you say, all you had was [name of defense counsel] notes. You didn't see him. You didn't read the police report. You didn't call him. You didn't come to Houston to visit him. Additional to what?

❖ ❖ ❖

PROSECUTOR: Additional to what?

A: Well, to all of the transcripts of the police reports and transcripts of interviews and photographs and video lineups and things that were sent to me that I did review.

Q: And you got all of that from [name of defense counsel]?

A: Or members of his office, yes.

Q: I guess that means that obviously that everything that was provided to you was provided by the defense?

A: Yes.

❖ ❖ ❖

Q: You talked about some 28 cases of the Department of Justice where it turned up that later people had been wrongly accused; is that right?

A: Yes.

Q: Twenty-eight cases?

A: Yes.

Q: And you found out or they found out that those people were wrongfully accused because of scientific evidence, right?

A: DNA evidence in particular.

Q: Well, that's scientific, isn't it, Dr. Loftus?

A: It's a form of scientific evidence, yes.

Q: So, I guess that means logically that the only way to ever know for sure if the witness is right is if you have any kind of scientific evidence that corroborates or backs it up, right?

A: You can have other forms of corroborating evidence that can exonerate the memory.

❖ ❖ ❖

Q: You're absolutely right. You could also have the fact that another witness corroborates what the first witness says and that's not really scientific, right?

A: Assuming the other witness is truly an independent witness, that could be a form of corroboration.

Q: Since you never met [name of an eyewitness] and you never met [name of another eyewitness] and [name of another eyewitness], you don't know how independent they are, do you?

A: I don't need to necessarily meet them in order to learn information that might relate to the extent to which they are independent or not.

Q: You're sure not trying to tell this jury that you think they're dependent on each other, do you?

A: Depends if they were interviewed by common people. If one person in common fed information from one to the other, if they were exposed to common media coverage, if they were exposed to the same materials, they may not be strictly independent.

❖ ❖ ❖

Q: You also know under the laws of our state, an expert witness from either side is allowed to sit in the courtroom while the other side is putting on their case. You've done that before, haven't you?

A: I've occasionally watched court testimony, but I don't know what the rule is in Texas.

Q: So, if you wanted to watch the testimony of [name of an eyewitness], [name of another eyewitness], and [name of another eyewitness], you could have sat right here on the front row and watched every bit of it, couldn't you?

DEFENSE COUNSEL: That's asking for a legal conclusion. It's an argument.

THE COURT: That's overruled.

Q: [By the prosecutor] Did you ask if you could do that?

A: No, I didn't.

Q: Did [name of defense counsel] ever ask you to do that?

A: No, he didn't.

Q: Because if you would have sat here during all their testimony, you would have been able to answer the question, "Was there any common media coverage between [name of an eyewitness] and [name of another eyewitness] and [name of an eyewitness]?"

and you would know the answer to that, wouldn't you, if you had sat here through it?

A: I don't know if I would or not.

Q: Because you didn't hear their testimony?

A: I don't know what they said on that point.

❖ ❖ ❖

Q: [By the prosecutor] Did you ever ask [name of defense counsel] whether or not he had any evidence that [name of an eyewitness] had been biased by the media before he identified this defendant [pointing to the accused] in a photo spread? Did you ever ask that question?

A: I did, as about media coverage and when the photographs were shown and when the media coverage was . . .

Q: Thank you for helping me, but my question was . . .

❖ ❖ ❖

Q: [By the prosecutor] My question was, "Did you ever ask [name of defense counsel] if he had any evidence that [name of the eyewitness] was exposed to the media before he picked out this defendant in the photo spread?"

A: I believe that we did discuss that, yes.

Q: Did you ask him that question?

A: I don't remember if I asked it as a question, but I do believe we discussed that issue because he told me about the massive coverage of this case in the regular newspapers and a weekly newspaper. So, we had that discussion.

Q: You wouldn't make an assumption because this was a high-pub case, that a witness like [name of the eyewitness] would let himself be exposed to all that? You would not assume something like that without talking to the man, would you?

A: I don't think I ever testified that he absolutely was exposed to that or not.

Q: You also told us that you testified over 230 times. I guess the meter's ticking. Is this 231?

A: Approximately.

DEFENSE COUNSEL: Judge, I object to the side-bar remark, meter's ticking.

THE COURT: That's sustained.

❖ ❖ ❖

Q: In those greater than 230 times, tell us again how many times you testified for the prosecutor anywhere in any state.

A: Well, of the criminal cases, I've testified once—I was called by the prosecution once to testify in a jury trial.

Q: Did they pay you?

A: Yes.

Q: One time out of 230?

A: Well, no, ma'am, because the majority of those are civil cases in which I might testify for the plaintiff or defense, depending on who was requesting the testimony.

❖ ❖ ❖

Q: Do you know of any eyewitness identification expert in the whole world who's more expensive than you?

A: More expensive? I do know experts who testify on memory issues who are much more expensive than I am, yes.

Q: Well, Park Dietz, I think, $500 maybe. Lenore Taylor [phonetic], $450. Colin Ross, I think, from Dallas is maybe $500 approximately. These are just estimates of what I've heard in their involvement in other cases.

❖ ❖ ❖

Q: I saw you looking through my boxes on the break. Did you see your books in here?

DEFENSE COUNSEL: Hold on. That's not correct. May we have the jury removed?

THE COURT: Excuse me. No. If you'd step up here, please.

[At the bench, on the record.]

PROSECUTOR: She did it.

DEFENSE COUNSEL: No, she didn't. I was with her the whole time.

THE COURT: That is a side-bar comment, and I just instructed you not to make side-bar comments. You can ask whether she looked in the boxes. Do not make side-bar comments like that.

PROSECUTOR: Okay.

THE COURT: Do you understand?

PROSECUTOR: Ask Matt?

DEFENSE COUNSEL: That's a false accusation.

THE PROSECUTOR: No, it's not.

THE COURT: She can ask the witness whether she did look.

PROSECUTOR: Ask Matt.

[Conclusion at the bench.]

PROSECUTOR: Dr. Loftus, did you see in my boxes your books?

A: As I was walking by, I couldn't help but notice that you had a huge collection of my books in that box because the spines were just standing out.

Q: Did you count them all?

A: I didn't count them, no.

Q: Five of them. And I've read them all, and I want to talk about this one first. *The Myth of Repressed Memory*, that's one of your books, is it not?

A: Yes.

Q: This is the first *Eyewitness Testimony* book?

A: 1979, yes.

Q: And I think the reprint would be this one, *Eyewitness Testimony*?

A: Correct.

Q: And then there's *Memory*?

A: Yes.

Q: And *Witness for the Defense*?

A: Yes.

Q: Does it surprise you that I would have them?

A: All five of those, a little.

❖ ❖ ❖

PROSECUTOR: Let's talk about *Witness for the Defense* first of all, okay? Do you remember your dedication, your dedication in your book? "We dedicate this book to the women and men in prison who have been wrongfully accused, convicted, or who have otherwise suffered because of faulty eyewitness testimony." Is that right?

A: I believe so, yes.

Q: Do you remember your acknowledgments in your books? You "owe a great deal of thanks to the defendants, their family members, lawyers, investigators, jurors, and others whose lives were caught up in these tragic dramas." You remember that?

A: I don't remember the exactly . . . nine years old, that book, so . . .

Q: You testified in the Ted Bundy case, did you not?

A: I testified in one Ted Bundy case, a case involving Ted Bundy, yes.

Q: And there's, I think, a chapter dedicated to Ted Bundy in this book, is there not?

A: There's a chapter about the case in which I was an expert witness, yes.

Q: And I think somewhere in the chapter, you say that you won't take a case unless . . . one of the requirements is you have to believe the defendant is not guilty or innocent. Your words. You have to believe the defendant is innocent and the defense lawyer has to tell you that he's innocent or you don't take the case?

A: That's not true.

Q: That's not in this book?

A: Well, I don't think I said it that way because it isn't true. I mean I would prefer to testify on behalf of people where I think there's a strong probability that they're innocent; but it isn't always true.

Q: In the Ted Bundy case you mentioned the part of the trial where it upset you that he smiled at the prosecutor. Do you remember that part of the book?

A: I don't remember the exact details. That was 25 years ago.

DEFENSE COUNSEL: Excuse me. Excuse me. Relevancy, Judge. I think this is irrelevant to compare one case with another.

THE COURT: Step up here, please.

[At the bench, on the record.]

PROSECUTOR: It goes to show her bias and her agenda. Her whole life is nothing but her position of . . . all of these people and how they're wrongly accused . . . and I intend to go through every one of these where it makes her feelings known. She has a mission in life, and this is her mission in life.

DEFENSE COUNSEL: I object to comparing cases. I think that's improper, and the reason it's improper is because the jury here doesn't have all of the evidence or all—it's like asking this jury to try other cases to determine whether it was a right or wrong result. And to compare other cases and the more sensational they were the more they want to compare them. It's not a proper comparison.

PROSECUTOR: They brought up all the books she's written. They introduced the 30-page vita with these names on them. So, I get to talk about the books.

THE COURT: I'm going to let you go into some talking about the books because I know you can get into her writing, but I'm not going to let you go through every single book that you have.

PROSECUTOR: Oh, I'm not.

THE COURT: You can make your point in maybe one or two things, but you're not going to go into every single one of them. You can make your point, and then you're going to move on, and I will stop you.

[Conclusion at the bench.]

PROSECUTOR: In the Ted Bundy case, you mentioned in your book about how you were offended or upset that at one point he smiled at the prosecutor. You remember that part in your book?

A: Well, that trial was in 1976. I'm sorry. My memory is very dim of him, but he did smile in a funny way, I thought, at the prosecutor. I have this memory of that.

Q: And your point of that was that it upset you because you went on to talk about how, to you, someone who's really innocent would be all upset and worked up at the prosecutor and, to you, the fact that Ted Bundy managed to smile at the prosecutor showed that he was guilty, and you were upset that you had testified for a man you then believed was guilty because he smiled at the prosecutor?

A: That's not true.

DEFENSE COUNSEL: Object to argument. Side-bar remarks. I object to the form of the question.

THE COURT: That's overruled.

PROSECUTOR: You don't remember saying that in this book?

A: I don't know if he did that particular crime or not. I don't know. I didn't know then and I. . . .

Q: No, ma'am. My question was: "You don't remember writing that about the smile to the prosecutor in the Ted Bundy chapter in this book?"

A: You'll have to show me where I said that.

Q: When I get to that sticky, I'll show it to you. You also testified in the case of Angelo Buono and Kenneth Bianci [sic], the "Hillside Stranglers."

DEFENSE COUNSEL: This is the problem of comparing the cases. We object to it. It's not proper.

THE COURT: Sustained.

Q: [By the prosecutor] Did you write in your book on page 9, *Witness for the Defense*: "Judges often view me as an unnecessary complication and only reluctantly accept my testimony. They claim that some expert testimony invades the province of the jury or that I offer jurors little more than commonsense information." Did you say that in your book?

A: You'll have to show it to me.

DEFENSE COUNSEL: It's not relevant, Your Honor. It's not relevant to . . . and I object to the side-bar comments to my objection.

THE COURT: I'm sustaining on the side-bar comments and overruling your objection.

PROSECUTOR: Your book, page 9.

A: Yes, I wrote that.

❖ ❖ ❖

Q: Okay. And did you write this paragraph right here: "My fellow psychologists are in bitter disagreement about the appropriateness of expert testimony. My opponents argue that my research is unproven in real-life situations and my testimony, therefore, is premature and highly prejudicial." You wrote that in your book?

A: Yes.

Q: "Victim's rights groups accuse me of tampering with truth and justice."

DEFENSE COUNSEL: I object, Judge. The prosecutor is just going to read.

THE COURT: Sustained.

PROSECUTOR: I'm not going to read the whole book, Judge.

THE COURT: I'm sustaining his objection.

PROSECUTOR: This part right here about opponents, other psychologists and psychiatrists argue that your research is unproven in real-life situations, do you see that sentence right there?

A: I think I was referring to a couple of people at Johns-Hopkins University [sic] with that remark.

Q: Okay. And those people and whoever you would be referring to by this remark "real-life situations" because obviously you say in your book, "You can never exactly recreate a real-life traumatic event like a stabbing or a murder," can you?

A: Well, not ethically, no. That's why we have to look at actual cases and also do the experimental work and look at the collection of data together.

Q: And the experimental work basically boils down to you having some of your college students come in and watch a film and then, after the film, you ask them a bunch of questions.

A: That happens in some of the studies.

Q: Like you said [a] while ago, the film about the little boy whose head got shot at the end of the bank robbery, that was a film?

A: It was, yes.

Q: So, there's no way you can know for sure what witnesses would do in a real-life situation because you can't scientifically recreate that type of event?

A: Well, we certainly can't subject witnesses in the experiments to, you know, a whole lot of trauma that might harm them. That's why we have to do what we can in the experimental studies and complement the analysis with actual analyses, with real-life cases.

Q: You can sure never get close enough to something like being stabbed 14 times or watching someone be murdered. You can never come close to that?

A: Not experimentally, no.

Q: And the people who criticize your experiments are other psychologists?

A: Sometimes, yes.

Q: And other psychiatrists?

A: Occasionally, yes.

Q: People whose opinions you respect?

A: Sometimes I do, yes.

❖ ❖ ❖

Q: Have you ever read any of the reviews of your books?

A: Sometimes, yes.

Q: Isn't it true that there's a review of one of your books where the person says . . .

DEFENSE COUNSEL: Excuse me. That's a criticism by a reviewer. I object to it.

THE COURT: That's sustained phrased that way.

PROSECUTOR: Let me show you in this same book, *Witness for the Defense*, page 12, this highlighted two sentences right here. Did you write this?

A: Yes.

Q: "I needed to be alert, wholly in the present moment."

DEFENSE COUNSEL: Excuse me. Just because she wrote it doesn't make it relevant. She's cherry-picking little portions of the books. It's improper. It's not proper cross-examination. Doesn't go to the merits of her testimony. It doesn't go to what she said in this court. It's improper cross-examination. Personal attack.

THE COURT: The way the question is phrased, I sustain the objection.

PROSECUTOR: Read this sentence to yourself, please, Dr. Loftus.

A: Okay.

❖ ❖ ❖

Q: Isn't it true basically that it is your position or thought process every time you come into a criminal court that you believe a man's future can depend on your testimony?

A: Well, it's not always a man; but I do feel that it's important to take this very seriously, yes.

Q: Because a defendant's future could depend on your testimony?

A: It's not just one person's future. It's many people's future.

Q: But based on all the books of yours that I read, anyway, your concern is always for the defendant?

DEFENSE COUNSEL: That's a statement, not a cross-examination. We object to it.

THE COURT: It's overruled.

A: That's not true.

PROSECUTOR: Did you ever have any concerns or voice any concerns in any of these books about the victims?

A: I don't know about exactly in those, but I've certainly written about victims, including recently over in the Bosnia war trials.

❖ ❖ ❖

Q: Talking about lineups for a minute. Defense counsel asked you some questions about the lineups in this case. Did you see the video-taped lineup?

A: Yes.

Q: From page 24, when you described grossly suggestive lineups in this book, you talk about a lineup where they had a black suspect in the lineup with five white men.

That's a suggestive lineup?

A: Very.

Q: And you talked about one where the suspect was six-foot-three and everybody else in the lineup was under five-foot-ten. That's a suggestive lineup?

A: Yes.

Q: You also talked about one where the offender was in his teens and he was in the lineup with all people over the age of 40. That's a suggestive lineup?

A: Yes. Those are some extreme examples.

Q: And you talked about police officers maybe insinuating or hinting things to witnesses. On page 25, if an officer looked at a witness after a lineup and said something like, "Take another look at No. 4," that would be a hint or suggestion, would it not?

A: Yes.

Q: And maybe while the witness is looking at the lineup, if a cop leaned over and said, "What do you think about that one?" that would be a hint or suggestion?

A: Yes.

Q: Were you in the courtroom during Sergeant George Anderson's testimony?

A: No.

Q: How about Investigator Mike Williams'?

A: No.

Q: Are you going to be here this afternoon when Steve Slater testifies about the photo spread?

A: I don't know. Depends on how long you question me.

Q: And basically you told us that you testify in cases where eyewitness identification is the sole evidence against the defendant?

A: Sometimes that is true, yes.

❖ ❖ ❖

Q: Usually there isn't any type of scientific testimony or evidence in the cases you testify in?

A: Sometimes there is.

Q: Is there in this case?

A: Well, from what I've heard, it's disputed evidence.

Q: Who told you that?

A: One of the attorneys.

Q: Which one?

A: I don't remember.

Q: What is disputed exactly?

DEFENSE COUNSEL: Well, I object to that. That's improper cross-examination.

THE COURT: Sustained.

PROSECUTOR: What is the nature of the scientific testimony?

DEFENSE COUNSEL: Excuse me. That's far beyond the scope of direct examination. It's asking her to comment on things that she was not asked about.

THE COURT: It's overruled. She can answer if she can or say that she doesn't know.

THE WITNESS: And the question again, Your Honor?

PROSECUTOR: What is the nature of the scientific evidence in this case going to be?

A: I had heard there was going to be a big dispute over whether there were fibers present. Some say there's fibers present and some say no fibers, no match for fibers. That's what I'm referring to.

Q: What type of fibers?

A: I really don't know.

❖ ❖ ❖

Q: When was it that this book came out?

A: 1991.

Q: You say in this book that, at the time, you had been called in to testify as an expert seven times, and in only three of those was the testimony permitted in court; is that correct?

A: Well, that's not true in 1991; but it may have been true at the time of the particular case, if it was in the early 1970's, it might be true.

Q: Isn't it true that you also say in your book that there are times when you want to testify because . . . not just because of the potential for mistaken ID, but because you also believe your research on memory needs to get out of the laboratory and into a real-life forum where it might make a difference? Didn't you say that on page 76 of your book?

A: Well, I don't remember the details of that, but I do feel that this kind of research that I and others have done is relevant to helping real people, and I'd like to see that happen. So, if that's what you mean by that or if that's what I meant by that, I still agree with it.

❖ ❖ ❖

Q: Let's talk about stress. You speak about a continuum of stress, something about, as the stress begins to build, then it would affect someone's ability to remember what happened. And then you say, when they're moderately stressed is when you would expect fairly optimal performance. Am I saying that right?

A: Well, you're describing the Yerken Dodson Law which I present in that book. It basically says that under low arousal, as when you're waking up in the morning, or very high arousal, our performance, mental functioning is impaired somewhat. There's this middle area where we're performing at our best.

Q: For the court reporter's benefit, you spell Yerken Y-e-r-k-e-n; is that correct?

A: Right and Dodson D-o-d-s-o-n.

Q: So, if you had interviewed [eyewitness], you would know at what level his stress level was, would you not?

DEFENSE COUNSEL: Objection. Objection. I could state it better at the bench, Judge.

THE COURT: It's overruled.

DEFENSE COUNSEL: Well, my objection is they wouldn't let us talk to [name of the eyewitness].

THE COURT: That's overruled.

PROSECUTOR: Do you know at what level of stress [eyewitness] was when he wrote down the license number and saw the defendant leave the wig store?

DEFENSE COUNSEL: I object to the form of the question because that's not what he said.

THE COURT: Ask it again. I'm sorry. I didn't hear it.

PROSECUTOR: Do you know at what level of stress [name of the eyewitness] was when he saw the license plate number and wrote it down when he saw the defendant leave the wig store?

DEFENSE COUNSEL: Object to that, Judge. [Name of the eyewitness] at best says 80 to 90 percent.

THE COURT: It's overruled. You may answer the question.

A: I mean, I assume that he was not highly stressed nor was he just waking up in the morning, that he was somewhere in the middle.

PROSECUTOR: So then, according to your own book, moderately stressed prior to that, you would expect fairly optimal memory performance. I mean, he wasn't the one being stabbed.

DEFENSE COUNSEL: I object to the side-bar remarks, Judge.

THE COURT: That's overruled.

PROSECUTOR: If [eyewitness] wasn't the one being stabbed, he wasn't under extreme stress, correct?

A: I don't assume he was under extreme stress, correct.

Q: If he was just curious and paying close attention, according to your book, he was what you would expect to find, fairly optimal memory performance from him?

A: Well, I do not expect to see him impaired by extreme stress under those conditions, no.

Q: Thank you, Doctor. No further questions at this time.

DEFENSE COUNSEL: Nothing further. May the witness be excused?

THE COURT: Yes. The witness is excused. We're going to take a break now.

Ladies and gentlemen, I remind you to remember your admonitions from the Court. Don't discuss the case among yourselves or with anybody else. If you would step back into the jury room, the bailiff will be with you in just a minute. The court is in recess.

To read the transcript with commentary by the Center for Criminal Justice Advocacy, go to *http://criminaldefense.homestead.com/Loftus.html#anchor_8*. The edited and annotated version is copyright Ray Moses, 2005.

APPENDIX 4

Examination under Oath Outline

Part of the preparation for any interview requires an outline of the information needed to achieve the results sought by the interview. Outlines, like the one that follows, are not scripts but ideas for the questions that need to be covered.

The direction of the interview changes after the first question is asked and should flow in a logical direction from the answer to the first question. Since much work was put into preparation of the outline, its questions are familiar to the interviewer and will not be looked at as the questions flow in a logical manner from question to answer to next question.

Only after the professional determines that he or she has obtained most of the information needed will the interviewer look at the outline to determine if any important subject was missed and if further questions are required.

1. The reason you are here is because, when you purchased your policy of insurance from my client you promised that, in the event you presented a claim and the insurer asked, you would submit to examination under oath. You have presented a claim, and you are here to testify as part of the investigation being conducted by my client. Although you have taken the oath and the court reporter is taking down everything that is said today, this is not a deposition which can only be taken in a lawsuit. We are not adversaries; we are only attempting to get as many facts as possible under oath.

2. Can you read the English language?
3. Can you speak any English?
4. Have you ever been known by any other name?
5. Have you elected to have Mr. Attorney here as your attorney?
6. Are you the person most knowledgeable about the claims concerning the residence at 2211 Shadow Hill Way?
    a. If not, who is?
7. Who owns the property today?
8. Did you ever observe the damage that is the subject of your claim?
9. Who owned the property at the time you first noticed there was damage to the property?
    a. When did you first notice damage to the property that became the subject of your claim?
    b. What did you observe?
    c. What was the cause of the damage?
    d. Where was the damage when you observed it?
    e. Who lived at the residence when you first observed the damage?
    f. Who was responsible for the damage?
    g. Who was responsible for the repairs?
10. Did you observe any other damage?
    a. What?
    b. Where?
    c. When?
    d. How did it occur?
    e. Who caused the damage?
    f. Who first observed the damage?
11. Describe all damages that were repaired by you or on your behalf?
12. Describe all damages that were not repaired by you at the time of the sale?
13. When did you first acquire an interest in the property?

14. Did you ever live in the property?
15. What was the condition of the property at the time you acquired it?
16. From the date you acquired the property until you first presented a claim:
    a. Did you do any repair work to the property?
    b. As to each, state:
        i. When?
        ii. What?
        iii. Why?
        iv. Where?
        v. Who did the repairs?
        vi. How were the repairs performed?
17. From the date you acquired the property until you first presented a claim:
    a. Did you do any remodeling to the property?
    b. As to each:
        i. When?
        ii. What?
        iii. Why?
        iv. Where?
        v. Who did the work?
        vi. How were the repairs performed?
    c. What did you do to maintain the property?
        i. Did you have a regular plumber?
        ii. Did you have a regular carpenter?
        iii. Did you have a handyman?
        iv. Did you have a property manager?
18. What is your occupation?
19. Are you employed?
    a. By whom?
    b. What is your position?
    c. What is your salary?

d. Did you have any active involvement with the property on Shadow Hill Way?

e. If not, who did?

20. Did you have any active involvement with the maintenance and repair of the property on Shadow Hill Way?

    a. If not, who did?

21. Did you have any active involvement with the rental of the property on Shadow Hill Way?

    a. If not, who did?

22. Did you have any active involvement with the sale of the property on Shadow Hill Way?

    a. If not, who did?

23. Did you have any active involvement in obtaining insurance for the property on Shadow Hill Way?

    a. If not, who did?

24. Did you sign an application for insurance?

25. Did you read the application before you signed it?

26. Did someone translate the statements made in the application to you so that you were certain the responses were accurate at the time of the application?

27. You made sure the statements of fact on the application was [sic] true, didn't you?

28. You knew, didn't you, that the insurance company would rely on the statements you made in the application before deciding to insure or not insure you?

29. And all the statements of fact on the application were true, weren't they?

30. Have you read the policy on which you are making claim?

    a. Did you understand anything you read?

31. What other insurance do you have that was in effect on the first day you observed damage at Shadow Hill Way?

32. Have you ever had insurance similar to the insurance issued by my client?

a. When?

b. Who was the insurer?

33. Have you ever had a policy canceled?

34. Have you ever had a policy non-renewed?

35. Have you ever had an insurer refuse to insure you or property you owned?

36. Have you ever presented a claim to an insurer before this claim for loss to real or personal property?

37. Has any insurer suggested you obtain insurance elsewhere or they would be compelled to cancel or non-renew a policy it had issued to you?

a. Identify each:

38. Has any insurer ever declined to insure you?

39. What is your:

a. Date of birth?

b. Place of birth?

c. SSN?

d. Drivers' License number?

40. What is your residence address?

a. Do you live with anyone?

b. Who?

41. Marital status:

a. Have you ever been married?

b. Name of spouse.

c. Child(ren), names and ages.

d. Where do they live?

42. Have you ever been the victim of a crime?

43. From what high school did you graduate?

44. What colleges, universities, or trade schools have you attended?

45. What degrees or certificates have been conferred on you?

46. What licenses have you been awarded?

47. What licenses do you presently hold?

48. Are you certified by any professional association?

49. What real property do you own?

50. Do you have a checking account?

- **a.** Identify each:

51. Do you have a savings account?

- **a.** Identify each:

52. Do you own any stocks?

- **a.** Identify each:

53. Do you own any mutual funds shares?

- **a.** Identify each:

54. Do you own any bonds?

- **a.** Identify each:

55. What is your net worth?

- **a.** How was it calculated?
- **b.** What portion is art created by you?
- **c.** Have you ever had an independent person appraise or otherwise value your art?
- **d.** Do you have a Personal Articles Floater on your valuable personal property?
- **e.** Do you have a policy that insures your valuable personal property?
  - **i.** Identify the insurer:
  - **ii.** Identify the broker:
  - **iii.** What is the amount of coverage?
  - **iv.** What is the value?

56. Have you ever prepared a personal financial statement?

- **a.** When was the last one?
- **b.** To whom was it directed? [*demand copy*].

57. Have you ever applied for a real property loan on the Shadow Hill Way property or any other property?

- **a.** May I have a copy of the loan application?

58. List each of your continuing obligations, e.g.:

   a. mortgage payments.

   b. boat payments.

   c. credit union debts.

   d. child support.

   e. spousal support.

   f. judgments.

   g. liens, etc.

   h. debt payments.

   i. utilities.

   j. etc.

59. What is the dollar amount of the claim you are presenting to your insurers?

60. What is the cause of the loss or losses that are the subject of your claim?

61. Did you lose any rents as a result of the loss?

62. Did you sign a sworn statement in proof of loss?

   a. Here is a copy; did you read it?

   b. Did you have someone translate it?

   c. Are you certain the statements made in the proof of loss are true?

63. Have you intentionally misrepresented any facts to me today?

64. Did you misrepresent any facts to my client when you acquired the policy that is the subject of your claim?

65. Have you intentionally concealed any facts from me during this examination under oath?

66. Did you present this claim to my client with an intent to defraud my client?

About the Author

Barry Zalma, Esq., CFE, is the founder of Barry Zalma, Inc., a California consulting firm whose practice emphasizes consultation with, and testimony as an expert witness on insurance claims handling, insurance coverage, and insurance fraud for insurers, those in the business of insurance, and policyholders. Barry Zalma, Inc.'s clients included major insurers such as Lloyd's Underwriters and major law firms. Barry Zalma now limits his practice as a consultant and an expert witness for insurers, their lawyers, policyholders, and their lawyers.

Mr. Zalma writes the twice-monthly *Zalma's Insurance Fraud Letter,* which is available free of charge from ClaimSchool, Inc. and at www.zalma.com. He also publishes Zalma on Insurance, a five-day-a-week blog summarizing new and important insurance law appellate cases, and Zalma on Insurance 101, a video blog on insurance claims handling containing 1,022 videos.

Mr. Zalma writes a regular column on insurance for the *Underwriter Insider* and the *Insurance Advocate* Magazine. He was the host of the television series *Insurance Fraud,* broadcast by the Insurance Broadcast System and a contributor to WRIN.tv. In addition, he has written continuing education courses for A. D. Banker Company, WEB.CE, and Illumeo.com, which provide continuing education credits for insurance agents, insurance brokers, claims adjusters, public insurance adjusters, accounting professionals and chief financial officers.

Mr. Zalma has testified as an expert witness in the California Superior Court, the United States District Court, and the Superior Courts of Nebraska and Idaho. He is recognized as an expert on insurance claims handling, commercial general liability (CGL) policy, the comprehensive general liability policy, bad faith, insurance fraud, Jewelers' Block Insurance, and other inland marine coverage. Mr. Zalma has written, or rewritten, CGL, fire, auto, earthquake, Jewelers' Block, and other insurance policies for insurer clients.

Mr. Zalma is the first recipient of the first annual Claims Magazine/ ACE Legend Award.

In addition to membership in the American Bar Association and the California Bar, he is a member of the Southern California Fraud Investigators Association, the California Conference of Arson Investigators, and the International Association of Arson Investigators, and he has been awarded the designation Certified Fraud Examiner. He serves on the continuing education faculty of the Association of Certified Fraud Examiners.

Some of Mr. Zalma's books are available as Kindle books or paperbacks at Amazon.com and can be purchased at *https://zalma.com/blog/insurance-claims-library/*. His reports can be found on Tumbler at *https://www.tumblr.com/search/bzalma* on Facebook at *https://www.facebook.com/barry.zalma*, and you can follow him on Twitter at *https://twitter.com/bzalma.*

Prior to launching his legal career, Mr. Zalma was Senior Claims Representative with Fireman's Fund Insurance Companies, emphasizing investigation and adjustment of third-party and major first-party losses. Mr. Zalma also served as a Special Agent in Charge for U.S. Army Intelligence.

ClaimSchool, Inc.
4441 Sepulveda Blvd.
Culver City, CA 90230

Index